Better Homes and Gardens.

RENEWING
AN OLD HOUSE

BETTER HOMES AND GARDENS® BOOKS

Editor: Gerald M. Knox
Art Director: Ernest Shelton
Managing Editor: David A. Kirchner

Associate Art Directors: Linda Ford Vermie,
Neoma Alt West, Randall Yontz
Copy and Production Editors: Marsha Jahns,
Mary Helen Schiltz, Carl Voss, David A. Walsh
Assistant Art Directors: Harijs Priekulis, Tom Wegner
Senior Graphic Designers: Alisann Dixon, Lynda Haupert,
Lyne Neymeyer
Graphic Designers: Mike Burns, Mike Eagleton, Deb Miner,
Stan Sams, D. Greg Thompson, Darla Whipple, Paul Zimmerman

Vice President, Editorial Director: Doris Eby
Group Editorial Services Director: Duane L. Gregg

General Manager: Fred Stines
Director of Publishing: Robert B. Nelson
Vice President, Retail Marketing: Jamie Martin
Vice President, Direct Marketing: Arthur Heydendael

All About Your House: Renewing an Old House
Project Editor: James A. Hufnagel
Associate Editor: Willa Rosenblatt Speiser
Assistant Editor: Leonore A. Levy
Copy and Production Editor: Mary Helen Schiltz
Building and Remodeling Editor: Joan McCloskey
Furnishings and Design Editor: Shirley Van Zante
Garden Editor: Douglas A. Jimerson
Money Management and Features Editor: Margaret Daly

Associate Art Director: Randall Yontz
Graphic Designer: D. Greg Thompson
Electronic Text Processor: Donna Russell

Contributing Editors: Jill Abeloe Mead, Stephen Mead
Contributing Senior Writer: Paul Kitzke
Contributors: Denise L. Caringer, Cathy Howard, Jean LemMon,
Leonore A. Levy, Willa Speiser

Special thanks to William Hopkins, Bill Hopkins, Jr.,
Babs Klein, Scott Little, John Mikovec, and Don Wipperman for
their valuable contributions to this book.

RENEWING
AN OLD
HOUSE

INTRODUCTION

Every old house has a story to tell. One may have been home to three or four generations of farm families, then abandoned when the farm was no longer workable. Another old house may have been erected by a prosperous merchant and later converted into a rooming house. A third might have had more humble beginnings—as worker housing constructed by a railroad or factory, for example—and now sits amidst a new/old neighborhood straining at its bootstraps.

Many of the millions of old houses in this country have something to say not just about the past, but about the present and future as well. This book is dedicated to them, and to people with the vision, courage, and stick-to-itiveness needed to make an old house new again.

Renewing an Old House covers all sorts of old houses, from gracious Colonials and Victorians to 1950s tract homes. If you've just recently caught old-house fever and are wondering where to start, this book can introduce you to the kinds of prospects you're likely to come across. It also will help you determine which is right for you. If the house you'd like to renew is one you already own, *Renewing an Old House* can tell you what to do with it.

Here you'll find advice about planning a renovation or restoration, case studies about what others have done, where to get financial aid for what you'd like to do, how to deal with interiors and exteriors, information about mechanical systems and the specialized parts you'll need, and how to decorate for now without losing track of then.

In short, *Renewing an Old House* applies home improvement and decorating to houses with a history. Other volumes in the Better Homes and Gardens® ALL ABOUT YOUR HOUSE Library can supplement the ideas and information presented here. We hope this book and its companions will prove valuable resources and inspiration as you seek to improve your present home or find a new old one.

RENEWING AN OLD HOUSE

CONTENTS

CHAPTER 1

IS RENEWING FOR YOU?   6

Do you really want to live in an old house?
Can you see the potential in a Cinderella house?
Should you restore or renovate?
Can details be saved?

Can you recycle a commercial structure?
Can you live with the mess and uncertainty?
Can you handle the economics?

CHAPTER 2

BEST BETS FOR RENEWING   20

First considerations
The city row house and its cousins
The urban recycling project
The close-in Victorian

The suburban classic
The newer suburban house
The small-town cottage and the house on a farm

CHAPTER 3

FINDING THE "RIGHT" OLD HOUSE   34

Where do you want to live? Beginning the search
Where do you want to live? A neighborhood checklist
Visual inspection: Exteriors

Visual inspection: Interiors
Research: How to do it, where to go
Money matters

CHAPTER 4

PLANNING A RESTORATION OR RENOVATION   46

Getting started: What you'll encounter
Sizing up the project
Getting the existing house down on paper
Determining wants and needs

The design process
Final design choices
Nailing down costs
Getting the work done

CHAPTER 5

WHAT OTHERS HAVE DONE: NINE CASE STUDIES   66

Working from within
Adding on
Re-creating the past
Making a plain house pretty
Reviving a row house

Making less from more
Converting a shop into a home
Bringing new life to an old farm
Renewing an entire neighborhood

CHAPTER 6

RENEWING EXTERIORS 84

Faithful restoration
A renovation that raised the roof
A renovated ranch house

Paint: Color and contrast
Special details deserve special attention

CHAPTER 7

RENEWING INTERIORS 98

Down with walls for a bold new look
Something old, something new
Redirecting traffic
Ceilings
Stairs

Windows and doors
Fireplaces
Old woodwork
Contemporary millwork

CHAPTER 8

UPDATING MECHANICAL SYSTEMS 118

Heating and cooling
Wiring

Plumbing

CHAPTER 9

KEEPING UP APPEARANCES 130

Hardware
Lighting
Interior details

Exterior details
Wood floors
Wall treatments

CHAPTER 10

FINISHING AND FURNISHING 142

Planning room arrangements
A restored house

A renovated house
A remodeled house

WHERE TO GO FOR MORE INFORMATION 155

ACKNOWLEDGMENTS 157

INDEX 158

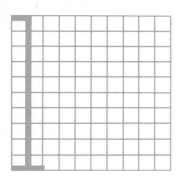

IS RENEWING FOR YOU?

Old-house people are a special breed. Whether or not you're among them depends on where and how you want to live, your interest in history and architecture, your stamina and sense of adventure, and your pocketbook. If you're thinking about buying an older home in need of renewing, or considering renewing the home you already own, this chapter presents some points to ponder. Finding the perfect place to live is never easy. Deciding what constitutes the perfect place for you and your family is an even more fundamental challenge. Once you've determined that you want something other than a brand-new house, a number of decisions still remain.

DO YOU REALLY WANT TO LIVE IN AN OLD HOUSE?

Not everyone wants to live in an old house—but for those of us who do, the question quickly becomes "which old house?" If you're lucky enough to have found a charming, affordable older home that's always been well cared for and has recently been rewired, replumbed, and redecorated in colors that you, too, would have chosen, you are one of the lucky few.

More likely, you'll be faced with a home that needs new paint, new wallpaper, and at least a few improvements that cannot be considered simply cosmetic. Besides visual appeal and nostalgia, you need to think about structural integrity, a watertight roof, energy efficiency, plumbing, and wiring, too.

The house you're thinking about renewing may be the one you're already living in. If not, the search for a renewable old house can take many forms—and many months, as well. Where you want to live, what size and vintage home you think you can best deal with, how much money and time you have, and a host of other factors will determine what you'll finally find.

Happy house-hunting

Sometimes you can stumble onto the perfect house by accident, in the course of a walk through an appealing neighborhood or a drive on a winding country road. Or perhaps there's a special home you'd like to own, but it's not currently for sale. If you're really interested, keep an eye on it.

The owners of the midwestern farmhouse pictured *opposite,* for example, had driven by the house several times and admired it before it came on the market. By the time it became available, it was already an old friend.

To help put your thoughts in order, first decide where you want to live. If you're looking at an urban neighborhood that is just beginning to come back into its own, your chances of finding a house that needs little more than tender loving care are not as good as they might be in a more established setting. For an introduction to house types and their relationship to neighborhood considerations, see Chapter 2—"Best Bets for Renewing."

Decorator specials

With lots of looking and some luck, you may well be able to find an older home that needs only minor work and continued care. Money is a factor, too. A house in good condition will require a larger initial outlay, but the advantage is that once you've paid the purchase price, you won't have expensive repair projects to wrestle with.

For many people, redecorating is the fun part of renewing, but even cosmetic changes don't occur overnight or without careful planning. To see how three families redecorated their very different renewed homes, see Chapter 10— "Finishing and Furnishing."

A considerably more ambitious undertaking than the decorator special is the "handyman special." To renew one of these, you'll need considerably more than decorating expertise and funds. In fact, you may need to develop a very discerning eye just to find one. More about this on the following page.

CAN YOU SEE THE POTENTIAL IN A CINDERELLA HOUSE?

Some houses have charms that have been obscured by decades of neglect and ill-chosen "improvements." Identifying one of these requires a measure of X-ray vision to see how the house once was— and a crystal ball to envision what it could be again.

The picture-pretty Queen Anne Victorian shown *at right* needed considerably more than a fresh coat of paint when the present owners purchased it a few years ago. Clapboards were hidden by asbestos siding, the gingerbread trim and porch railing were missing, and the attached gazebo was in a state of collapse. Besides all that, the roof leaked and many of the leaded glass windows were cracked and loose in their frames.

The owners knew there was a treasure buried here, however, and undertook a major restoration. First they installed a new roof and made the gazebo level and upright again. Then they had the stained glass repaired and the original gingerbread duplicated. Finally, they highlighted everything with period-pink paint.

As you're evaluating an old house, bear in mind that problems you *can't* see may be even more costly to correct than those you first notice. Wiring may date back to the early-light-bulb days and be nowhere near sufficient for today's needs. Fixtures may be in poor condition and plumbing lines leaky. The furnace may be a converted coal-burner that uses far more fuel than it should. Lack of insulation may mean that even with the furnace working at peak efficiency, the house just doesn't stay warm.

Most of these problems are solvable, but they take time, money, and effort—sometimes more of all three than you bargained for. To find out more about what to look for when you're considering how much work a renewing prospect will need, see Chapter 3—"Finding the 'Right' Old House"— and Chapter 4—"Planning a Restoration or Renovation."

SHOULD YOU RESTORE OR RENOVATE?

"Renewing" is a broad term. It can mean scrupulously *restoring* a home to its original state or completely *renovating* it by gutting the interior and creating a new house within the shell of an old one. Whether you should restore, renovate, or amalgamate the two approaches depends on a variety of factors.

The very Victorian entrance hall pictured *opposite* is a classic example of ''interpretive restoration''—bringing a home back to something that *might* have been its original appearance. Here the new version is perhaps a bit brighter and more luxurious than the original, but the mood and period basically match the home's original life.

If the older home you're planning to renew has architectural or historic qualities that you value or that would be hard to re-create in all-new construction today, then some degree of restoration is probably the best choice. You may want—or be required by local ordinance—to preserve at least the exterior of your home, or to keep it consistent with others in the area.

If there's very little of the original left, complete restoration may be an expensive and difficult option. Then your best bet is to renovate, perhaps using period furnishings and architectural details to help create a mood of the past.

The high-gloss, stripped-down interior shown *at left* is in a house down the street from the one whose front hall is featured *opposite*. This home had been converted to a duplex, and in the process, most of its period charm was lost, so the owners chose to completely renovate the interior.

If you're contemplating a renovation, be warned that many renewers strongly believe home owners have an obligation to preserve the past. Discussing your plans with an architect, neighborhood group, or preservation society may help clarify your thinking.

To see a range of renewed homes, from a restored farmhouse to a renovated commercial structure, turn to Chapter 5—''What Others Have Done.''

IS RENEWING FOR YOU?

CAN DETAILS BE SAVED?

Details of all kinds, from leaded glass to fluted pilasters to multicolored octagonal slates atop mansard roofs, are the soul of historical architecture. To many people, details are among the most important reasons old buildings are worth preserving. If details are in a state of decay or disrepair and you want them back, you may have to rebuild them or replace them with similar items. If you're planning a renovation, and old-time charm isn't a major factor in the design scheme, you may still feel an obligation—for the sake of architectural character, history, or sentiment—to preserve some details.

When it comes to old buildings, the question of what to preserve involves both taste and conscience. If you've purchased a fine old home that's rich in detail, there's little point in doing anything but preserving it. It's a document of the past. You're more likely to find, however, that some exterior elements are cracked or missing, the woodwork is obscured by layers of paint, and plaster rosettes that adorn the ceilings of half the houses on the block are mysteriously erased from your dining room and parlor.

If restoration or renewal with a period flavor is your ambition, preserving or replacing as many details as possible is a clearcut goal. You may be able to rebuild them, find replacements at salvage or antique shops, or order reproductions from an ever-increasing number of specialty suppliers. For more about deciding what to keep and how to keep it, see Chapter 4—"Planning a Restoration or Renovation"; to learn more about re-creating or finding what you need, see Chapter 9—"Keeping Up Appearances."

It's possible, of course, that there may not be much left to preserve. If that's the case, and a renovation in the spirit of today and tomorrow is what makes sense for you, you may still want to hold on to something for the sake of history or character—maybe a mantel that has somehow survived the home's boardinghouse phase, or ornate exterior woodwork hidden for years under asphalt siding.

To see a range of successful solutions for handling details—or the lack of them— see Chapter 6—"Renewing Exteriors" and Chapter 7— "Renewing Interiors."

IS RENEWING FOR YOU?

CAN YOU RECYCLE A COMMERCIAL STRUCTURE?

Cities and towns are constantly changing. The industry and commerce that swept over an area a century or more ago may have outgrown its original buildings, been left behind by technical and economic progress, or simply be in need of newer, more up-to-date spaces. As businesses and industries move from the center city to outlying areas, they leave behind sturdy old factories and warehouses, as well as smaller buildings that housed retail trade. The structures are sound, the interior spaces often dramatic. If they're no longer needed for or well suited to their original purposes, they may offer exciting possibilities for residential recycling.

The spectacular loft pictured here occupies an upper floor in what was once a warehouse on Boston's Commercial Wharf. As the photo *above* indicates, one of the building's attractions is its fine view of Boston's harbor. Like many other buildings overlooking the harbor, this one has been recycled—individual spaces are sold as residential condominiums.

The owners of this space spent six months shaping the loft into a home, doing much of the work themselves to keep costs down, but turning to a professional designer and a licensed contractor for expert advice and assistance. An L-shaped balcony, pictured *at left,* serves as the master bedroom and den. The relatively low-ceilinged area below this loft-within-a-loft houses the bath and laundry area. The variation in ceiling height not only allows for dropped ceilings and recessed lighting but also helps partition the space subtly, without losing the sweeping appeal that's half the charm of any loft.

The planning and work you'll need to do to recycle a commercial structure have a lot in common with recycling an old residence, but there are significant differences, too. For example:
• You'll need to make sure that zoning ordinances and building codes allow for converting the space to residential use.
• Wiring, plumbing, and other utilities may need more work to bring them up to living standards than would be the case in a structure originally planned and built for residential use.
• If you're truly pioneering in an area where few people have been living, lending institutions may be reluctant to provide financing.
• Besides generous floor space, high ceilings, and unusual architecture, you can expect another advantage if you decide to purchase commercial space for residential use: Cost per square foot is often much lower than for comparable residential space.

For more about converting commercial space into living quarters, see pages 24-25 and 78-79.

CAN YOU LIVE
WITH THE MESS
AND UNCERTAINTY?

Even putting down a
new kitchen floor or re-
papering a bedroom
causes a few days of
dislocation, mess, and
anxiety. Multiply this
many times over, and
you have a general idea
of what it's like to redo
an entire house. Strip-
ping exterior shingles,
repairing leaky roofs,
updating utility lines,
patching plaster, stain-
ing new woodwork to
match old—these are
just a few of the myriad
entries on the list of
things to do. Careful
planning is the key to
getting through it all as
painlessly as possible.
Don't plan dinner par-
ties for the day after the
kitchen is supposed to
be finished. Instead, be
realistic about how
much time and talent
you have to devote to
the tasks, and how
much money you can—
and want to—pay oth-
ers to do jobs for you.

The would-be dining room pictured *above* is actually a well-swept, tidied-up-for-the-camera example of what a room looks like when it's in the midst of being restored. It took weeks of patience, hard work, and cleanups to reach the handsomely eclectic state illustrated *at left*.

If you do not plan to live in your home while the work is being done, all you need to do is be sure the time frame you've worked out for keeping your former place is flexible enough to allow for delays in getting the future home ready. If, however, you are planning to renew your present home or expect to move into a new (to you) old house and fix it up while you live there, be sure you know what you're getting into. It will be wonderful when you're done, but difficult until then. Here are a few pointers that may help smooth the way.

• Kitchen remodeling is one of the most common parts of any old-home fix-up. Don't try to work around the mess. Plan on a series of carry-out or restaurant meals, if necessary; bring a toaster/oven, countertop broiler, or microwave into the family room, if possible, so you can do at least minimal cooking.

• Try to keep at least one room free of renewal mess and clutter, as a refuge from other rooms that may be barely habitable.

• If you have pets or small children, consider letting them visit relatives or close friends during times of maximum activity, such as knocking down walls or sanding floors. In addition to keeping kids or pets out of the way, it will protect them from exposure to possible hazards such as dust or toxic fumes.

• If heating systems need the kind of work that may put them out of service for a day or more, consider having the work done in warm weather; the longer daylight hours of the warm seasons are an advantage, too, if you'll be without lights for a while.

These are just a few of the many considerations involved in the decision whether to renew and, if so, to what extent. For more about planning and scheduling work, see pages 48-53; to learn about the mechanics of renewing a house, see Chapter 8—"Updating Mechanical Systems."

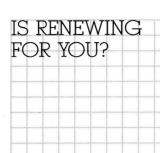

IS RENEWING
FOR YOU?

CAN YOU HANDLE
THE ECONOMICS?

Buying a house of any age is usually a major financial undertaking. Buying an older home in need of renewing presents additional economic concerns, such as getting financing for the whole package, not just the purchase itself. Happily, there are ways to offset the economic burdens.

One of the most intriguing aspects of buying a home in need of renewing may be the opportunity to help bring a neighborhood back to life. This challenge may take its toll, however, when it comes to getting financing. Banks and other financial institutions may balk at the area you've selected. Government programs, on the other hand, may go out of their way to encourage resettlement. For more about getting financing, see page 45; to learn more about tax incentives, see page 75.

When you're considering buying any building, keep in mind that the neighborhood's fate may be a key to your financial future. The stability of an already-settled neighborhood or the improvement of a neighborhood in the midst of renewal will affect how much money you'll make if and when you sell the home. For more about judging the quality and direction of a neighborhood, see pages 34-37. Ask yourself, too, whether there is any income potential other than resale: Can you rent an apartment, or use part of the structure for business purposes?

Once you own the property, you will have a whole new set of expenses to deal with. Consider the costs not only of aesthetic improvements such as painting the exterior, refinishing interior woodwork, and removing or strengthening upstairs partitions, but also of the things that don't show. However, you may not have to deal with them alone. The owners of the row houses pictured *at left*, for example, were able to benefit from the Tax Reform Act of 1981, which allows a 15-year depreciation period for improvement costs as well as a rehabilitation tax credit.

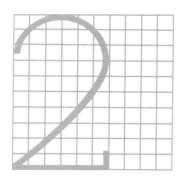

BEST BETS FOR RENEWING

One couple's wonderful old farmhouse is another's windswept relic in the middle of nowhere. One family's row house treasure is another's inner-city shoebox with not enough yard for the kids to play in. When you're looking for a house to renew, think of life-style as well as architectural style, the amount of time you want to spend working on the house, and the length of time the house has been standing. The renewal project that's right for you also has as much to do with where that house is located as with what it looks like. In fact, as you'll discover in this chapter, *where* a home is often determines what it looks like.

You've outgrown your apartment, looked at builders' houses, priced condominiums, and perhaps spent a whole season of weekends looking at houses that don't say anything to you. You know you want to find a new place to live, a place you can commit yourself to, but for aesthetic, financial, or other reasons, the usual possibilities don't seem very satisfying.

Renewing an old house may be the answer—but what sort of old house? Do you dream of restoring a battered inner-city row house to its former glory? Would you rather renovate a turn-of-the-century "white elephant," take two floors for your own, and rent out the third? Or would you be content to find a suburban home that still functions fairly well but needs a new heating system and cosmetic updating?

What can you find— and where?

Where you want to live has a lot to do with what you'll find. Sprawling Victorian homes, for example, built in the days of large families and abundant household help, are likely to be found in near-downtown areas of older cities, or in smaller towns that prospered during the late nineteenth century. Row houses, with two or three rooms per floor and two or three floors stacked atop each other, are primarily, but not always, inner-city finds.

Particularly if you will be moving from one type of environment to another, now's the time for some serious self-questioning. If you live in the outer suburbs and are considering moving back to the city, for example, ask yourself if being close to work, shopping, and cultural activities means as much to you as privacy and

outdoor space for gardening. A city house puts you much closer to your neighbors than you may be accustomed to. On the other hand, if you've always been a city person, ask yourself if you have the inner resources as well as the financial ones to move to the country and revive an old farmhouse. Will all members of your family have adequate transportation to work and school? Do you really look forward to the greater independence that rural living requires?

How much work are you willing to do?

Renewing needn't be a grand, all-consuming passion. Certainly, if you aspire to a painstakingly restored Victorian like the Italianate version shown *opposite,* you can expect to commit several years and thousands upon thousands of dollars to the effort. But not all vintage homes cry out for a major overhaul. Choose wisely and you might well be able to find a house that needs nothing more than a series of summer spruce-ups.

Given sufficient time, energy, and money, you can do almost anything to the inside of a house to make it suit your family's needs. You can knock down walls if a floor plan is unworkable, add up or out if you need more space, and redecorate to your heart's content. But you have to start with the house that's right for you. On the next 12 pages, we discuss the exciting and varied renewal opportunities that different settings and different types of housing offer.

THE CITY
ROW HOUSE
AND ITS COUSINS

In-city housing almost always means lots of people in relatively little space. New high rises and old walkups form the basic fabric of many in-city residential neighborhoods, but there's another category of in-city dwellings that's much more houselike—the row house.

A row house can be of almost any age and architectural style. It might be a simple two-story brick structure built early in the nineteenth century, or, in another part of the same city, it may be a later, more elaborate dwelling, with terra-cotta trim outside and carved woodwork inside. Narrow, freestanding, Victorian-era, two-story homes, like the not-yet-restored example shown *opposite*, are distinguished from true row houses only because they don't have shared sidewalls.

If you're interested in newer housing, consider the row houses that dot post-World War I or II neighborhoods beyond the inner city. This new—and often ignored—generation of homes, like those shown *below*, frequently offers very good value if you're willing to forgo some of the architectural and historical extras you'd expect from an older house.

Living conditions

In just about any row house, the floor plan will be compact and vertical rather than spread out. Row houses are built on narrow city lots; interior dimensions reflect that. Windows typically are located only at the front and back of the house, except in corner or end houses. Land is generally limited to a small backyard and perhaps a postage-stamp-size front yard.

The condition of available row houses varies widely, from lovingly maintained one-family homes to rundown rooming houses. What will be available to you depends heavily not only on your budget but also on your city's economic and social history.

If the downtown area has always been a vital, thriving neighborhood and has been considered a desirable place to live since it was first built, you probably won't find many deteriorated inner-city row houses, although there may be some tucked into areas that have not kept pace with the rest of the city. But if you live in a city whose core has declined, entire neighborhoods may have slipped into decay.

If you are considering moving into such a neighborhood, there are certain things you should consider. Schools, services, and security are the basics. (For tips about how to judge an area, see the checklist on pages 36 and 37.)

Other conditions matter, too. If there are a lot of vacant buildings around, find out why. Look into any government or private agency plans for neighborhood rebuilding or demolition, whether for a freeway, a housing project, or anything else that will alter the area. If plans exist, they may have been shelved, but don't assume they've been forgotten.

THE URBAN
RECYCLING PROJECT

Row houses are not the only good urban candidates for renewal. In cities all over the country, sturdy buildings that once served other purposes, such as schools, factory buildings, warehouses, fire stations, or one-of-a-kind mansions, are being converted to contemporary residential use.

Many such buildings are too large for one-family living nowadays. Often these lend themselves to conversion to rental apartments or, increasingly, condominiums.

Because the function and floor plan of an institutional building or large-scale residence, such as the Queen Anne-style mansion shown *above* or the grand-scale Georgian town house pictured *opposite*, is so different from twentieth-century housing, this kind of recycling project is unlikely to be a restoration, even a loosely adaptive one. Thoughtful renovation, with some attention to preserving such period details as cast-iron fronts or graceful interior support columns, presents a more realistic possibility.

How much work must you do?

In some cases, you may be able to purchase raw space in a building that's in the process of being renewed and do the finish work yourself, or have it done to your specifications. In this way you get the challenge and satisfaction of being involved in renewing an older structure, without all of the responsibilities.

If you have sufficient financial resources, or want to put together an investment group, you may wish to purchase an entire building and undertake a renovation project. Keep in mind that because you are dealing with a building that has not always been put to residential use, you may need to make additional changes in order to turn the structure into an income-producing or one-family residential building. Many nineteenth-century factory buildings, for example, have only cold water lines and some were wired for direct-current electricity.

Unless you are very skilled or the project is quite modest in scope, converting an entire building from one type of use to another may be more than you should take on. If you're interested in group investment or group work, however, a large-scale recycling project could pose an exciting challenge.

THE CLOSE-IN
VICTORIAN

Just beyond the central business and residential districts of many towns and cities, there's often an "inner ring" of big, old houses. Depending on the age of the original downtown, much second-generation development of available close-in land—really the first suburbs—took place from about 1860 to 1910.

These late-nineteenth-century homes are called Victorians, but the term covers several styles and many regional variations. Among the most common are:
• *Queen Anne.* Elaborate, with turrets, balconies, varied combinations of exterior materials, such as shingles, clapboard, and smooth wood, all in one facade. The home shown *opposite* is an example.
• *Second Empire or Mansard.* Notable for its distinctive double-sloped roof; often topped with a central tower.
• *Colonial or Georgian Revival.* Rectangular and boxy, with relatively little ornamentation except for columns around the door or porch.
• *Italianate.* Several variations; one is a flat-roofed square home, like the one shown *at right,* with extended eaves, heavy brackets, and a cupola or dormer.

Much as the styles vary—and we've mentioned only a sampling—many of the close-in Victorians are very large. The amount of space and its arrangement, however, aren't always practical by modern standards. Interior space was taken for granted, but because the land the homes were built on was prime real estate, the lots were rarely as spacious as the houses' sizes would seem to call for.

Unless you're looking in an area that has already undergone some urban revitalization in the past decade or so, the large old houses you see near a city's center often look very different from their original state. Their character and charm may be obscured by deterioration or obliterated by the loss of architectural detail. Commerce and crowding may have eroded their residential character; or the residential nature of the area may have survived in a different form, with the houses turned into multi-family dwellings and fallen into disrepair.

Homes of this type offer many of the advantages of in-city living, but with more interior space than many row houses or urban recycling projects. If you're considering purchasing and renewing a close-in Victorian, here, in addition to the considerations discussed on pages 20 and 23 and in Chapter 3, are several things to think about.
• How much work does the house really need? Will it call for more time and money than you can give it?
• Do you want to restore the home to some extent, or simply make it livable again in a twentieth-century style? If you plan to change the exterior, are there any historical-district limitations that would prevent you from carrying out your plans?

• Is a Victorian a practical home for you and your family? Keep in mind that utility costs for a house as large as those shown here can be more than most families can handle.
• Once the structure is restored or renovated, what could you do with it other than live in it? Does it have income-producing potential? Does zoning allow other than one-family residential use? For example, can you rent out two floors as apartments and keep one for yourself? Does zoning allow for any commercial use? If so, you could start a retail business on the ground floor, or rent that floor to another shopkeeper.

BEST BETS FOR RENEWING

THE SUBURBAN CLASSIC

The older suburbs of most cities are full of homes that don't fit the popular image of houses in need of restoration or major renovation. They already have bathrooms and kitchens with twentieth-century conveniences. Their room arrangement is familiar—living room, dining room, kitchen, and hallway downstairs; three or four bedrooms upstairs; maybe a sewing room or butler's pantry; and adequate, if not ample, closet space. Gas, electricity, plumbing, and central heating were built into them from the start, although the furnace may originally have been coal-fired.

Houses like this vary in age according to the part of the country they're located in. In the early suburbs of the East and Midwest, the standard "older" suburban home was built from about 1890 to 1940; in the older suburbs of newer cities, however, the peak of building often occurred after World War I.

The sizes and styles of older houses in the suburbs vary tremendously. Some of the affluent suburbs are rich in sprawling old Tudors and Colonials that rival the earlier Victorians in size, although the suburban lots tend to be larger. In other suburbs, the older homes are smaller and the styles, although still varied, may not be as clear-cut. In some areas of the country, you may see four-square stucco homes with hipped roofs, low-slung bungalows with broad front porches, brick-and-timber English cottages, stucco or concrete mission-style homes with red tile roofs, or Colonial-inspired designs like the welcoming house shown *at right.*

Renewal considerations

Although some close-in suburbs have declined along with the inner cities they surround, most maintain their middle-class residential character. The houses rarely suffer from deliberate neglect. They may have been lived in for decades by one family, however, with maintenance growing lax as the years passed. Unless the home has been recently and skillfully brought up to date, it will probably need a lot of physical improvements to make it practical and energy efficient. These houses are prime candidates for renovation.

In addition to practical concerns about utilities and energy, some aspects of the floor plan and decor may not fit your family's way of life. You may, for example, want to remove walls to make fewer but larger bedrooms, replace an extra porch with a family room, or redo the kitchen to provide more counter space.

There are several factors, other than house and specific neighborhood, to consider when you look at a house in an older, relatively close-in suburb. You may find that lots, although larger than those in the city itself, are smaller than those in the newer, post-World War II suburbs. On the other hand, because you're closer to the city, it will probably cost less to get to work and shopping if you drive; in addition, good public transportation may still be a part of the town's appeal, as it was during the suburbs' early development. Look for an established neighborhood with tried-and-true services, schools, and fully developed amenities such as parks. You may not find an extraordinary bargain in this kind of setting, but you will get good value for your money.

THE NEWER SUBURBAN HOUSE

Perhaps most of the sub-urbs in your part of the country are of relatively late date and most of the construction was done in the 1950s and 1960s. Or maybe you don't work in your city's downtown core, but in an out-lying section or in the suburbs themselves. If either is the case, older, close-in suburban housing doesn't enter the pic-ture. Newer, but not new, housing may offer unexpected opportunities for renovation without the demands of restoring historic homes or the expense of revitalizing middle-aged ones.

Stylistically, some newer homes don't differ markedly from those built earlier in the twentieth century. You can find 1950s brick Colonials, such as the one pictured *opposite,* and 1960s half-timbered Tudors. But more often, you'll find distinctively post-World War II styles—the familiar ranches, split-levels, and a handful of architect-inspired contemporaries like the one shown *below.*

Material differences
Besides differences in style, you'll find differences in materials. For example, aluminum siding in place of clapboards; bathrooms with resilient rather than ceramic tile flooring; drywall partitions rather than plaster walls.

When you look at homes built 20-40 years ago, you are likely to find components more standardized than those in older homes. Door and window sizes and lumber dimensions probably will be uniform. There will likely be fewer architectural details. For example, you'll find flush, hollow-core doors rather than paneled solid-wood doors. Wiring probably can handle air conditioning, a clothes dryer, and the other electrical conveniences we take for granted in the 1980s.

The aesthetic qualities of many recent-vintage homes are something else again. Thousands of homes around the country were built in the era of pink kitchen appliances and aqua-tiled baths. These kitchens and baths still function well enough, but they may not be to your taste. Updating may therefore be as much a case of changing colors and materials as bringing in new technology. Fortunately, the condition of these houses usually allows you to do the work gradually, as economics allow.

Clearly, homes of this type call for renovating in a more subtle way than their older cousins. The structure may be sound, but the house as a whole may not quite work for you and for your family. For example, many 1950s homes have smaller kitchens than those built today. A major concern in renovating such a house might be to expand the kitchen, perhaps by incorporating part of a utility room or back porch, or by adding on.

Even an under-40 house that appears to be in good condition will have suffered some wear and tear over the years. Gutters may need fixing or replacing; furnaces, installed in the days of abundant, inexpensive fuel, may no longer be optimally efficient. Insulation is iffy; weatherproofing could need beefing up. In short, re-newing a not-very-old suburban home is a combination of bringing it into step with late-twentieth-century life-styles and repairing any parts of the structure that have begun to show signs of age.

THE SMALL-TOWN COTTAGE AND THE HOUSE ON A FARM

Finding the perfect small town and spending summer evenings on a gingerbread-trimmed front porch overlooking its tree-shaded main street is one version of the 1980s American dream. Turning an abandoned farmhouse into an idyllic retreat has a place in that dream, too.

The small towns and rural areas of America offer an abundance of old houses from every period. Some have been immaculately maintained for centuries; others have been abandoned for decades and are just this side of irretrievable decay. Most fall somewhere in between.

The part of the country you live in or plan to live in largely determines what you'll find in the way of housing styles and building materials. Just a few of the possibilities include:
• The classic New England clapboard or brick farmhouse, with its rectangular shape, front porch, and endless ells and wings.
• The compact Victorian cottage, built of stone, brick, or wood, and nestled on a small in-town lot. The Carpenter Gothic pictured *at right* is an example.
• The low-slung stucco ranches of the Southwest and the two-story stone farmhouses of such disparate parts of the country as German-settled areas of Texas and New Jersey.

Certainly a home in a small town or rural setting can share many of the characteristics of a suburban house of the same vintage. In fact, a house that was once located on a farm or in a small town may now be in a city or suburb that has grown way beyond its original bounds. (See pages 102 and 103 for more about a renewed farmhouse that's now in the midst of a city.)

Help from afar

There are differences, however. Unless your town is already involved in preservation or restoration activity, you may not have convenient access to other, similar houses—and their owners—to look to for inspiration and instruction. (Check with local and national organizations, such as the Small Towns Institute, which are concerned with preserving and revitalizing historic small-town environments. An address for the Small Towns Institute appears on page 157.) Also, because distances are greater than in more-settled areas, supplies may be harder to track down.

Many small-town and country houses, however, lend themselves to some degree of restoration. A late-nineteenth-century farmhouse or small-town home may have undergone relatively few changes since it was built, in contrast to a city house of the same age. If so, restoration is likely to be a matter of refurbishing and repair rather than extensive research and reconstruction of vanished pieces. (See pages 84 and 85 for the story of a farmhouse that was brought back to its original appearance and condition.)

Another consideration is land: You're likely to have more of it than in the city or suburbs. This is an advantage in terms of aesthetics and privacy; it's also a responsibility. Many rural and semirural areas have programs designed to help preserve their agricultural heritage.

If you're taking over an old farm and do not plan to continue it as a working farm, check with the Land Trust Exchange (see address on page 157), local extension agents, and other experts to find out how best to maintain the land.

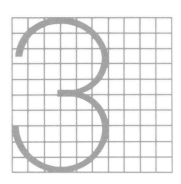

3

FINDING THE "RIGHT" OLD HOUSE

Where is it—the one old house you'd love to turn into a home? Too many prospective buyers wander into the market, stumble across a likely candidate, and snap the place up without thinking much about it. They may be rewarded later on, but then again, they may be sorely disappointed. It's a better idea to treat your search for an older home as a disciplined voyage of discovery, asking yourself general questions first about where and how you want to live and then zeroing in on individual houses.

WHERE DO YOU WANT TO LIVE? BEGINNING THE SEARCH

The first, and maybe the biggest, step in finding the right old house is deciding where you want to live. Country? City? Suburb? Small town? As you read in the preceding chapter, the choice you make goes a long way toward determining the type and style of house you're likely to find.

With this in mind, begin thinking in more detail about your family's style of living and how a change in location might affect it. Are you in love with the cultural and intellectual stimulation of big-city life? Have you ever lived in a large city? Or are you more attuned to the slower rhythms of suburbs, small towns, and country locales? Are your feelings based on experience, conversations with people who've lived there, or a vaguely defined sense that you'd like to try a new place?

What kind of neighborhood would you like to live in? Must you be close to work, schools, shopping areas, or public transportation? Would you prefer that your neighbors have incomes and backgrounds similar to yours, or do you think a more diverse population would add zest to your own life-style? Are you sold on the frequently rambunctious atmosphere of an urban environment? Or are you a nature lover, pining away for splendid isolation far from the madding crowds?

Consider big questions such as these before you start to narrow your selections to specific places. The owners of the remodeled Victorian farmhouse pictured *at right* considered their move from suburb to country at length. After they made that decision, they began to look at farmhouses in the area they had selected, with an eye toward good renewal prospects.

FINDING THE "RIGHT" OLD HOUSE

WHERE DO YOU WANT TO LIVE? A NEIGHBORHOOD CHECKLIST

What's the neighborhood like?" is one of those frequently asked questions that many aspiring homeowners only pay lip service to. Later on, when the deed is done and the house has become their home, they're often dismayed to discover that taxes are about to go through the roof, the trip to work is long and expensive, and the local schools are not up to par—or the one closest to home is scheduled to close at the end of the year. They *could* have known better.

The fact is, no house is an island—nor would you want it to be. Choosing the right town or neighborhood is as important as selecting the right home. To a significant degree, the price of any house will be determined by the quality and market value of other homes in the area. This fact of economic life not only will influence the mortgage you're able to negotiate but also will go a long way toward defining just how valuable your renewed house will be if and when you decide to sell.

At the same time, even homes that are potentially good investments may not be right for you if they're located in an area that doesn't match your family's style of living or are placed in a neighborhood where you can't live comfortably, economically, and safely.

Savvy buyers, then, choose a neighborhood *first*, before narrowing their search to individual houses. The following checklist should help you get started on the road home.

Rise and fall

Because houses are usually good investments only in relation to the health of the neighborhood around them, it's critical that you take the pulse of any area on your list. Is it deteriorating, relatively stable, or coming back strong?

Look for indications of a declining neighborhood. One smart way to start is by checking the recent sale prices of homes in the vicinity and comparing them to past transactions. The likeliest sources are local real estate agents and lending institutions, but a trip to the assessor's office (see page 43 for more about that) also may be in order. If you discover that prices in general are heading downward, or are just about stable at a time when inflation alone should be pushing them up, you can be fairly sure the neighborhood is on the skids.

Then take a sharp-eyed tour of the area—on foot. Pay close attention to the outward appearance of houses. Unkempt yards and poorly maintained structures negatively affect the value of every home in the neighborhood. Even if you buy a house at a bargain and turn it into a showplace, the return on your investment may be negligible—or nonexistent—if other homeowners around you don't follow suit.

As you're walking, look for small businesses and commercial outlets. A large and growing number often presage a neighborhood's decline if they're expanding into the residential area itself. But new commercial activity *near* a neighborhood may signal strength or revitalization.

When you're talking to local real estate experts, ask about rental activity in the vicinity. Owner-occupied homes are generally homes whose occupants have a commitment to the continued health of the neighborhood. If the number of renters is equal to or nearing the number of residents who own their homes, the neighborhood's market value may be slipping, especially if a small group of renters is rapidly becoming a large army.

Inquire, too, about the prevalence of crime against persons. (Police records, and often local papers, can tell you about this.) If muggings and other street crimes are on the increase, safety as well as property values may be a matter of concern. Crime against property, however, is also a constant in many affluent areas; it doesn't necessarily mean the value of homes is declining.

How eager are current residents to pack up and move out? Streets studded with "For Sale" signs may indicate a neighborhood's impending demise. But look into the reasons for the signs. A neighborhood with a large elderly population may be on the verge of a positive turnaround but filled with sellers eager to move to smaller quarters or warmer climes. On the other hand, the "For Sale" signs could mean something more serious—the discovery of toxic wastes in a nearby well, concern over increased noise pollution from a proposed freeway, or a host of other things.

Many older neighborhoods, which on the surface appear to be residential graveyards, have actually slid about as far as they're going to and are in the process of being revived. Deciding to renew a house in one of these areas could be one of the most profitable moves you'll ever make.

Look for signs of renewal. Talk to agents and lenders. Find out if federal, state, or local funds—or a combination of them—are being used to support attempts at revitalization. Check to see if an active neighborhood association exists and seek the advice of its members.

If you're able to identify a community on the rebound—before everyone else does—you may be able to buy a reasonably inexpensive house, one that you can renew confidently, and one that will increase in value as the neighborhood rejuvenates.

At your service

Never assume that every place has community services that will take care of your every need. Service quality and cost vary widely from area to area. Ask local officials, real estate agents, members of the local planning commission, and, most important, your neighbors-to-be for answers to the following questions:
• How good is police and fire protection? Gauge the distance between the departments and the neighborhood, and estimate the time it would take for help to arrive in an emergency.
• Where are the closest medical facilities? Choosing a neighborhood reasonably near a hospital or well-equipped clinic is generally sound advice; health care may be a crucial concern if one family member is likely to require expert assistance promptly.
• What utilities serve the area? Find out about their rates (which may, in fact, send you in search of another neighborhood) and the effectiveness of their service. Because utility bills are no longer forgettably small, now's the time to estimate approximate costs, rough as the calculations may be, and include them in your budget.
• What's traffic like? Are there well-enforced speed limits on streets around the neighborhood? Do trucks and buses, as well as cars, use the street? (Fumes and noise can be nuisances if heavy vehicles are

commonplace.) Is the procession of vehicles relatively light—or is the flow so continually heavy that children may be in danger when they're playing outside? Also check to see that streets are well-lit and potentially hazardous intersections properly controlled.

• How many kinds of public transportation are at your disposal? If you plan to rely on them heavily, are they conveniently near the area? Do they have affordable prices and suitable schedules?

• Where are shopping outlets located, and how many different types are easily accessible? Be aware of stores, such as supermarkets, that you'll use to supply everyday needs.

• How close are cultural attractions, places of worship, and sports stadiums?

• Are children well served in the neighborhood? Look for day-care centers, nursery schools, parks, and playgrounds, as well as recreational facilities for older children. Good day care and abundant parks attract young families, who may help revitalize or maintain neighborhoods.

• Is the neighborhood quiet? If not, do you mind the noise? Listen to the neighborhood at different times of the day. Houses near an airport, busy railroad tracks, or a major highway are no place for sensitive ears (and these features probably will hurt resale value).

Taxing matters

Community services, of course, carry a price, and homeowners pick up much of the bill in the form of property taxes. Where does all the money go? To finance local schools (usually the biggest chunk), to build and maintain roads, to install and service water and sewage systems, to pay for police and fire protec- tion, sometimes to provide garbage and snow removal, and to underwrite a broad range of special services and projects. Always check to make sure you know how the money is being allocated.

In any case, keep in mind that property taxes vary from area to area. As a rule, bills are higher in established neighborhoods where community services are well developed and are frequently much greater than they might be for comparable houses in a rural location. Nevertheless, the rate of periodic increases is ordinarily lower in older neighborhoods, especially in those counties or cities where there's a strong commercial and industrial base contributing tax revenues. Where that base is lacking, residents are often taxed more heavily to make up the difference.

Remember, too, that meager taxes aren't much of an advantage if they result in poor essential services. If you want to live in a neighborhood with superior police and fire protection, excellent public schools, and so forth, you'll most likely have to pay for them.

During your search, be aware of a few other factors that may influence your decision. Some communities slap new owners with an immediate increase in taxes. Often, there's not much you can do about it—except, of course, look for a place that doesn't.

Similarly, find out if property in the area is due to be reassessed soon. If so, the current taxes will almost always go up. It's a wise idea, as well, to get a feel for the local politics. Where major projects are in store—building a new school, for example—taxes may skyrocket a short time later.

Finally, would-be renewers must remember that all their good work is going to pay off in greater market value, which has at least one unpleasant side effect: steeper assessed valuation for the property and proportionately higher taxes. However, in some neighborhoods, particularly those urban areas that have hit bottom and are on the way up, you may be able to obtain temporary tax relief because political officials see an economic advantage to letting rehabbers do their work without additional financial burdens. Nonetheless, if the neighborhood renewal is successful, taxes will ultimately climb as property values increase.

Grading the schools

This is tricky business because schools are rarely rated, and few generally accepted standards are available for determining their quality. Seek advice from real estate agents, teachers, school administrators, other community officials, and neighbors-to-be with school-age children. Then, do a little scouting on your own.

Visit the schools your kids will probably attend, noting the quality and extent of the physical facilities, variety in the curriculum (with no skimping on basic subjects), qualifications of the faculty, number of extracurricular activities, and special services like guidance counseling and career planning. Drop in on several classes to observe how students and teachers interact. In addition, count pupils in each class. Many educators think there should be no more than 20 to 25 in the elementary grades.

If you're evaluating public schools, find out how much money the school district spends per year per student, and how much it compensates faculty members. Compare those figures to other districts. Money often does buy quality when it comes to education.

Standardized achievement tests don't tell the whole story, but they're at least a way to gauge educational quality. How do scores compare with those in other districts of similar size and type throughout the state and nation?

Find out if adequate transportation exists for children who need it. If there is a bus to ride, how long is the trip?

Building ideas

Any renewer with grand plans should be generally familiar with local zoning ordinances and building codes before moving into a home. Inquire about building restrictions or complex procedures that may delay or prevent work.

Check to see if the community has a planning commission. Is it active and effective, or does development seem to be taking place without any central control? Some communities limit new construction in residential neighborhoods to housing only—in some cases, *single-family* housing only.

Also look into plans for municipal or private construction in the area—new roads or an office complex, for instance— that may affect, positively or negatively, property values in the neighborhood.

Neighborly advice

People, of course, give a neighborhood its character. Not the least on your checklist should be talking to the folks who come with the territory.

Don't be shy. Walk around, introduce yourself to the residents, and find out their opinions about the place they call home. Take the time to ask questions about all the subjects described earlier. They know from firsthand experience what it's like to live there.

VISUAL INSPECTION: EXTERIORS

The years take their toll on even the sturdiest buildings. If you're committed to renewing an older house, you've already decided to spend time and money making a home better than it is. Even so, you should probably avoid buying property with pronounced structural deterioration or a collection of seemingly minor difficulties that, taken together, would be prohibitively expensive to repair. What's more, any exterior work can be costly, and you'd be wise to know roughly what repairs would cost before making an offer for the house.

One effective way to narrow down your choice of houses is to make a close visual inspection of the home's exterior. If you discover signs of trouble, call in a professional—a structural engineer, architect, or home inspector—for an assessment before the two of you go inside to check further. Here's what to look for.

• Sight down the sides of the house to ensure that the outer walls are plumb and square. If they are not, extensive—and expensive—repairs may be needed to correct an underlying structural problem.

• Look for cracks along the foundation walls. Any that are more than ¼ inch wide may signal serious damage; a pro will know for sure.

• What do window and door frames look like? If you spot any that are obviously out of square, exterior walls may be sagging.

• Also check windows and doors for warping, rotting, and cracking. Extensive problems often call for costly repairs. Look at the windowpanes, too. Cracks may indicate that the house is still settling.

• Using a pair of binoculars, inspect the roof for missing shingles, worn areas, and loose or rusty flashing. Obvious trouble here usually means trouble inside, such as water-damaged structural members and plaster. In addition, different roofing materials have varying life spans. Even if a roof looks all right on the surface, find out from a professional if you'll need to install a new one in the near future.

• While you're examining the roof, zero in on the chimney, looking critically at the flashing, mortar joints, and cap. Small areas of loose or crumbling material can be repaired without much difficulty, but if whole bricks are missing, the entire chimney may have to be rebuilt. Also check to see if the chimney has a flue liner. Without one, it's a definite fire hazard.

• Scrutinize exterior walls carefully. Inspect wood siding for rotting and splitting; small sections can be fixed easily, but large expanses of bad wood indicate that you'll probably have to re-side. If water has penetrated the walls, structural members could be affected, too. Masonry walls should be crack-free, with tight and solid mortar joints. Don't worry if it looks as though you'll have to do a little repointing, but disregard houses with a lot of crumbling mortar. Extensive mortar repairs are extremely expensive. Use a knife to poke at cracks or bulges in stucco siding. If the lath has pulled away from the building, the whole wall may have to be removed and restuccoed.

FINDING THE "RIGHT" OLD HOUSE

VISUAL INSPECTION: INTERIORS

If a house stands up to your exterior inspection, it's time to take an equally critical look at the shape of things inside. At this stage, the best advice is to hire professional help, if you haven't already. No matter how knowledgeable you are, or think you are, certain parts of an older home's interior—patched-onto electrical and plumbing systems, to name two—are often extremely difficult for an amateur to evaluate.

An impartial expert can give you a complete assessment, in writing, of the building's current condition and an informal estimate of how much you'll have to spend for repairs if you buy the house.

Here are some things you and your advisor should do.
• Check for sturdiness. Jump in the center of rooms. If one or more of the floors are springy, it may indicate sagging beams and joists. They can be strengthened, but the job is expensive.
• Poke structural members with a screwdriver or penknife to detect possible termite troubles. (Some states require an official inspection for termites before a home sale can be complete.) If you come across extensive termite infestation, forget the house and go on to another. Damage caused by carpenter ants and powder-post beetles, however, is usually less serious. In any case, an expert will be able to determine how widespread the problem is, if insects are currently chewing away at the wood, and whether or not it's worth your while to exterminate them and make the necessary repairs.
• Check all ceilings and walls for stains, peeling paint, and falling plaster. If moisture has ravaged large parts of the house, only expensive and extensive repairs will make them right again.
• Damage to the sill plate, caused by water or insects, is common in old houses; if it's widespread or extends to the house studs as well, you'd be better off searching somewhere else. In any event, ask a pro to examine this part of the house thoroughly.
• Assess the plumbing. Older homes often have a truly wacky array of patched-on pipes—so wacky that you can almost count on replacing all the supply lines. This is neither expensive nor overly difficult to do. Replacing drains, however, can put a big dent in your budget. To check quickly, pick out an exposed section of the main soil stack and give it a hard bang with the handle of a screwdriver. A clear ring indicates the stack is all right, but a dull sound, in most cases, means a new one needs to be installed. Turn on faucets throughout the house, running several simultaneously. Low water pressure could mean you'll need to bring in a new water line from the street.
• Like the plumbing, the electrical system is likely to be a maze of patched-on additions. Expert advice is essential. Generally speaking, if the house hasn't been rewired in the last 30 years, figure on doing a comprehensive electrical overhaul.
• Check the furnace. If it's been converted from coal to gas or oil, you'll want or need to replace it at some point—probably sooner than later. Furnaces *can* survive well over 50 years. Even if they're fully operational, however, older heating plants are frequently energy-wasters. Right at the start, it's often wise to budget for a new furnace and water heater with energy-saving features built into them.

FINDING THE "RIGHT" OLD HOUSE

RESEARCH: HOW TO DO IT, WHERE TO GO

Every house has a story to tell, an intriguing record of facts and figures that helps to define the way it was at various times in the past. When you've narrowed your *search* to a specific neighborhood or particular house, and are ready to think about restoring or renovating, you'll probably have to do some *re*searching by following a trail of information back through time and constructing a mini-history. Aside from satisfying basic curiosity, research will help you find out what the home and neighborhood used to look like.

Government work
The assessor's office is a likely place to start. County or local agencies have one very good reason for keeping comprehensive records of even the oldest structures: The records help to determine property taxes. (In some locales, your quest may lead to a department of records or vital statistics, a planning commission, or some other governmental body rather than an assessor's office.) No matter where you find it, most of the material should be available for the asking. Although you can't take files out of the office, you can usually make photocopies at nominal cost. Because you may be spending several hours there, it's wise to call ahead for an appointment.

What you'll discover is a treasure trove of information about each dwelling in the area: the initial cost and who originally owned the house and land, the home's architect and builder, zoning at the time of construction, and subsequent owners and the purchase prices they paid.

Many offices keep more detailed records, including a copy of the building plans; a precise description of the materials used; and, in certain cases, one or more photos of the house when it was first added to the tax rolls.

Keep searching
Look into other, more general, sources, as well. Go to the city, county, or state historical society, and ask for local histories and old town directories; they can be invaluable research aids.

Similarly, libraries and historical societies frequently keep newspapers for decades and collections of vintage photographs. Although many newspapers, particularly the larger ones, guard their photo morgues jealously, you may be able to search through them, too.

At the same time, don't neglect the growing number of books and magazines devoted entirely to the restoration or rehabilitation of old homes. In addition, the U.S. Department of the Interior is a major source of information on the subject. (See pages 155 and 156 for a listing of helpful publications and organizations.)

One of the most useful organizations is the National Trust for Historic Preservation, a nonprofit organization based in Washington, D.C. Both the national association and affiliated local memberships provide advice and support to owners and would-be owners of historic homes.

Don't spend every minute reading and looking on your own. Get involved with a historical or preservation society and talk to those in the know about the area's older houses. In some localities, historical groups sponsor tours that let you see firsthand what other people have done to bring their homes back to life.

FINDING THE "RIGHT" OLD HOUSE

MONEY MATTERS

When you're trying to finance the purchase of a renewable home, you have twin tasks ahead: finding money both for the purchase itself and for the remodeling, restoration, or renovation.

These are, in the eyes of most lenders, two entirely different business propositions, even though you may view them as one and the same. If you qualify for a conventional mortgage, securing purchase money is usually no problem because the lender has substantial collateral—the house. However, short-term construction loans are much riskier because, if your plans fall apart, the lending institution may be left with lumber, nails, and an unfinished job. Consequently, interest rates for loans of this variety are generally higher.

Fortunately, in recent years, banks and savings and loan associations—the two biggest players in the home-financing game—have become more willing to accommodate individuals who need money both to buy and remodel.

Combine and conquer

Combining elements of long- and short-term financing is frequently the best way to latch onto the required funds. Today, there are many options. It certainly pays to shop around, but some of the most common include:

• Combining a loan for both the property and the construction from a single lender, but in two stages. This means getting interim funds at one interest rate during renewal and then permanent financing at a lower rate once the work is done.

• Arranging the financing to buy the property from one lender and, at the same time, getting a written commitment for more capital when the construction is completed. With this commitment, you then talk to other lenders and obtain the construction money as a personal loan at a higher rate. When the renewal project is completed, the initial lender assumes the financing at the lower level of interest.

• Negotiating what lenders call a "takeout." One institution lends the money for both property and construction at a higher rate. A second lender then buys the loan package from the first and reduces the interest rate when the work is over.

• A less complex arrangement—for lenders, anyway—involves negotiating a series of standard home improvement loans, in amounts of up to $10,000, once you've purchased the property. Although this strategy lowers monthly payments considerably, you ordinarily have to pay off each loan before you can get another. If interest rates go up in the meantime, you could end up shelling out a lot more than you otherwise might.

Total private financing is by no means your only alternative, especially if you're planning to buy and renew a home in a once-declining urban neighborhood. The federal government, through its Department of Housing and Urban Development, offers several interest-subsidy programs, as do many states and some cities. If you qualify for one or more, you may be able to get money at rates well below the market level.

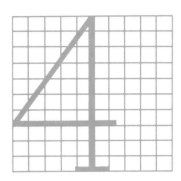

PLANNING A RESTORATION OR RENOVATION

Welcome home! At this point, you may be asking yourself and everyone around you, "How did I get into this?" But don't worry. Planning a restoration or renovation is one of the most satisfying parts of renewing an older house. This is the time to let imagination be your guide—a time to put your dreams on paper and see if they'll really work. Then, once you have a workable plan, you can start to turn your dreams into reality. In this chapter, we'll show you how one family of renewers explored several options and then selected the one that was best for their house—and for them.

GETTING STARTED: WHAT YOU'LL ENCOUNTER

Now that you've found an older home with possibilities, or decided that your present house fills the bill, the logical question is: What next? How do you go about transforming an aging dwelling into the best possible home for your family? Should you preserve, restore, renovate, or do a little of everything?

Ultimately, the answer will depend on your own vision, enthusiasm, sense of style, and particular needs, limited always by the size of your pocketbook. At the outset, be sure the definitions of and distinctions between the various types of renewal are clear to you.

• *Preservation* is a somewhat passive policy, one that usually involves maintaining a structure as it is and halting further deterioration without making major alterations in design or function. Unless you own a historically valuable house in fairly good condition, this is unlikely to be the best approach for you.

• *Restoration* is a studied attempt to return a structure, inside and out, to the way it was or might have been. Strictly accurate restoration requires that changes made over the years be undone and any missing features replaced. Many restorers take a less rigorous view, however. For reasons of comfort, convenience, or economics, they choose to carry out an interpretive restoration, which returns a building to the spirit if not the letter of an earlier time.

• *Renovation,* sometimes referred to as *rehabilitation,* is a present-minded plan that relies on contemporary standards and techniques to make an old building usable or livable again. Although renovation may call for tearing down parts of the original structure or demolishing modifications made in the past, good renovation respects the past. Renovation should not be confused with wholesale remodeling, which may involve stripping a building down to the bare essentials and ignoring the past. A good renovation will try to preserve or restore important architectural features as long as they don't seriously compromise the building's newfound practicality.

It's often possible to combine elements of each solution—for example, preserving or restoring a building's exterior and renovating the interior.

Past, present, future
Regardless of which route you take, try to cultivate a sensible view of the large task ahead before you get down to the details. No old house will ever be new again, and few restorers or renovators can afford to strive for perfection every step of the way. Learn to make reasonable compromises as you plan. And remember that even the most sensible plan inevitably fails to account for all potential problems.

The owners of the home pictured *opposite* knew that whichever renewal route they took, a lot of time, money, and work would be involved. The house had started life as a single-family dwelling and had been converted into a two-family side-by-side. Since the new owners' goal was to turn it back into a one-family home, preservation was not an appropriate option. The choice lay between interpretive restoration and full-scale renovation. Starting on page 50, you'll see how the owners considered plans and possibilities for the two alternatives.

SIZING UP
THE PROJECT

If you've just purchased a house, you know from the prepurchase inspection and engineer's report that your home is fundamentally sound. If you've lived in the house for a long time (or inherited it) and have any doubts about its structural integrity, now is a good time to check your home's mechanical and structural health.

Once you've assured yourself that the building is likely to be around awhile longer, you can start thinking about its future. First, put your priorities in order and take a closer look at what needs to be done.

A good way to start is by thinking about how the interior and exterior might look if they were fully restored or renovated. Consider how rooms might appear with years and years of anachronistic modifications removed and the major sections restored to their original look and function. Or think about how living spaces would work if old walls were torn down and new passages opened up.

Take along a notepad as you go from room to room and backyard to front yard. Make rough sketches of any ideas you have. At this point, don't worry about how you're going to do the job, just about what the results will be like. Note all the existing features you think you'd like to keep or repair, including things such as ornamental plasterwork, stained or leaded glass, original light fixtures, carved moldings, bathroom fixtures, and so forth. Before heavy-duty construction or destruction begins, you'll need to carefully remove these items or place protective coverings on them.

Make note of landscaping features, too. If there are large

trees and shrubs, or well-established flower beds and other plantings, keep in mind that these take years if not lifetimes to replace. Try to avoid damaging roots with heavy construction equipment.

Remember as well that it's a good idea to know what your yard looks like at every season of the year before you make any drastic changes in it. Don't cut down trees, prune bushes, or pull up plants unless you're sure you know what you're getting rid of. The big old shrub that looks so dreary in

late fall may be a mass of brilliant blooms in May and a foliage highlight of your garden all summer long.

Advice to rely on
The U.S. Department of the Interior offers a set of standards that can help just about all well-intentioned old-house renewers, whether their goals are preservation, restoration, or sensitive renovation. Here is a summary of those standards.
• Do not destroy distinguishing characteristics. Changes that have occurred over time may have acquired significance in their own right. Recognize and respect them.
• Regard any building as a significant product of its time,

worthy of respect as a monument to social history if not fine architecture.
• Make every reasonable effort to use the building for its original purpose.
• Handle distinctive stylistic features or examples of skilled craftsmanship with sensitivity.
• When possible, repair rather than replace deteriorated features. If replacement is unavoidable, the new material should complement the old in design, color, composition, texture, and other visual and tactile qualities.

Windows and doors—both exterior and interior—may need to be made more energy efficient and modified to function more smoothly. Ideally, windows and doors should be plumb and should operate without excessive jamming. Old wood frames, such as those shown opposite and above, almost always need repair or reinforcing. If you can avoid replacing them, you stand a better chance of keeping the mood and style of the home's original period intact.

Check all openings for energy efficiency. Do the windows move when you push them? Is there a draft coming in around the window trim? Many older houses need basic weatherproofing—caulking, weather stripping, insulating— although most residential buildings built before the 1940s are more energy efficient than their younger counterparts, partly because builders concentrated on bringing in natural sources of light, heat, and ventilation.

The radiator shown above is just one part of an antiquated heating system. Mechanical and electrical systems often must be made more efficient, as well as brought up to code. This often means updating extensively—or replacing completely. Older heating systems, even when structurally sound, often gobble fuel; aged plumbing systems frequently require brand-new supply lines; and old electrical service usually needs upgrading. Expert evaluation is invaluable.

In pre-World War II structures, all original walls will be plaster, although there may be partitions that postdate the originals and are made of drywall. A few minor cracks in plaster, even extensive hairline cracking, are easy to fix, as long as the cracking is not a symptom of continuing foundation problems. Pay particular attention to the condition of plaster detailing, like that shown above. Repairing details of this kind may call for skilled professional assistance.

GETTING THE EXISTING HOUSE DOWN ON PAPER

Before you can plan changes, you need precise and detailed knowledge of the house as it currently exists. The best way to acquire this knowledge is to note and record spatial relationships and structural characteristics on paper.

Original drawings and sketches, if you have them, are invaluable, as are renderings of remodeling projects that were done over the years. Often, your community's building department will have a fairly complete record of your home's physical history.

Even if you're able to find a set of original construction plans, it's a good idea to take your own measurements and put together a set of up-to-date drawings with dimensions you are sure about. Although you'll need a professional to do finished drawings, especially for a whole-house project, you can provide your own rough sketches for smaller-scale projects if you feel your measuring and graphic skills are up to the task.

Inch by inch
Using the proper tools and techniques, such as those pictured *at right,* measure each room in the house, rounding off dimensions to the nearest half-inch. Then use these numbers to draw room-by-room outlines on tracing paper taped over graph paper, allowing ¼ inch for each foot of actual space.

Next, measure individual openings and design features—windows, mantel projections, alcoves, and so forth—on the rough drawings. Also note which way doors open and where wall switches, electrical receptacles, and heating/cooling system registers are located.

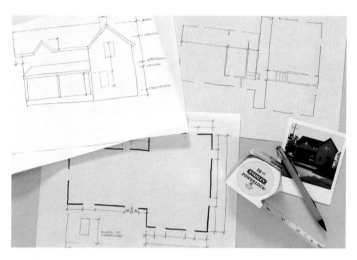

You'll need an 8½x11-inch pad of ¼-inch graph paper; one or two well-sharpened, soft-lead pencils with good erasers; masking tape; inexpensive tracing paper; and a 16-foot heavy-duty measuring tape. Most interior walls are about 6 inches thick, so allow a half square for each wall's thickness. Work carefully as you're roughing out graph-paper plans. If you're off by only one square, your room will appear a foot larger or smaller than it really is.

Have someone help with holding the tape, to make sure it's completely taut, and double-check each figure before writing it down. Always measure to the very edge of a structural element, as shown here. Include the height and width of door and window openings and the distance between them. One good way to check your figures is to total the individual dimensions along each wall to see if they add up to the surface's overall height and width.

For outdoor work, you may want to use a 50-foot tape. After you have the overall dimensions, concentrate on measuring exterior elevations—the height of door and window openings, the vertical distances between windows, the height from the ground to the sill line (as shown here), and so forth. Also record the dimensions of architectural features such as roof overhangs and dormers.

Follow a similar procedure for the home's exterior, but start by photographing each side of the house. Then take down overall dimensions and measure specific structural features, paying particular attention to the height of eave lines and the height and width of door and window openings. With the photos as your guides, rough out scaled sketches of each side, adding the interior position of floors and ceilings as you go along.

When you've finished this step, turn your attention back inside, using the data on the separate room drawings to produce rough floor plans also accurately drawn to scale on tracing paper.

Now you can turn over your data to a design professional, who will be able to translate everything into a set of finished floor plans, exterior elevations, and other pertinent elements. At this stage, you needn't call in a full-fledged architect, although that may be advisable later. For drawings of this kind, you can turn to knowledgeable contractors, architecture students, or house designers without formal architectural backgrounds.

The picture *above* shows finished floor plans of the two levels of the house featured in this chapter. The building's side-by-side, two-family design is clear from the existence of two kitchens on the main floor, two staircases, and two large second-floor baths.

DETERMINING WANTS AND NEEDS

Whatever direction you're considering for your renewing project, now is the time to begin filling in details, on paper, about the things you want to do or have done. Think of this as a wish list. Include items in general order of importance, but don't leave something out just because it seems too expensive or too trivial. You may be able to lay the groundwork for a major change so that it can be done conveniently and economically later. Similarly, a change that seems minor may become much more serious if other work doesn't take it into account.

If you're planning a restoration program, you'll need to find out as much as possible about both your home's history and the general architectural and furnishing styles of the past. Keep in mind that in an interpretive restoration, alterations that are functional and personal are often made even if they don't relate directly to the history of the house.

As the notes shown *at right* indicate, many restoration projects are determined as much by your family's needs as by the home's original layout and appearance. For example, the owners of the house featured in this chapter wanted more outdoor living space than it offered when they purchased it. They wondered whether, in the restoration process, they could re-create something that might have been part of the original one-family nature of the house. Because their restoration would be interpretive rather than exact, they could modify the past to make an outdoor living area suitable to their own needs.

RESTORATION

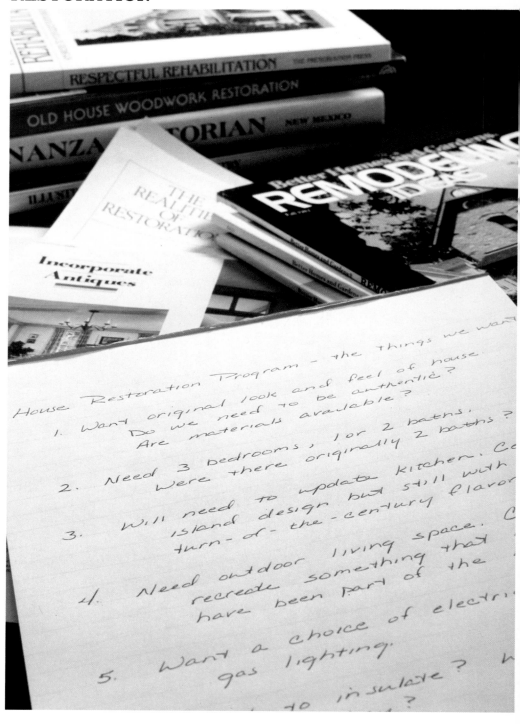

House Restoration Program – the things we want
1. Want original look and feel of house. Do we need to be authentic? Are materials available?
2. Need 3 bedrooms, 1 or 2 baths. Were there originally 2 baths?
3. Will need to update kitchen. Ce island design but still with turn-of-the-century flavor
4. Need outdoor living space. recreate something that have been part of the
5. Want a choice of electri gas lighting.
   to insulate?

RENOVATION

Even if renovation rather than restoration is your goal, you may not need a totally original scheme. Instead, you may decide to base at least some of your plans on the home's original design, using what still works for you and changing what does not. For example, as point 2 of the notes shown *at left* indicates, the owners of the house liked the original roofline, but also were thinking about an addition, which would change the home's shape. Even with an addition, they hoped to maintain some of the roof's original lines.

The list here also incorporates some less basic, more dream-oriented possibilities. Point 5, for example, suggests a patio or deck off the family area. This is an updated version of the "outdoor living space" asked for on the restoration wish list. Similarly, the new eat-in kitchen, possibly with serving bar, goes beyond the purely functional.

Even in a restoration, however, the kitchen and baths are unlikely to be ideal in their original state. These are rooms that you may well decide to change substantially, even if you are preserving much of a home's original quality.

In planning a renovation, you'll want to collect as many ideas as you can. Besides making your list of desired features, dig into books and magazines devoted to renovating and remodeling. Talk to others who've undertaken projects of this magnitude. All the while you're browsing, be on the lookout for approaches you can use in your own home.

THE DESIGN PROCESS

When it comes to developing interior and exterior design changes, you'll probably want—and need—expert advice. The more you know about the basic tools and concerns of the process, the better and sooner you'll be able to contribute your own ideas and reach a mutual understanding. Working with an architect or house designer on a whole-house renewal will probably involve looking at a series of sketches and plans until you arrive at the best approach.

The restoration plans pictured *at right,* for example, include porch columns of a style quite different from those shown on pages 58 and 60. Both styles would have been suitable for a period restoration, but the owners felt the rounded columns were more cohesive design features than the fretwork-flanked, squared-off fluted columns originally planned. Similarly, the facade in the renovation plan shown *opposite* reflects an early stage of design thinking. In later drawings, there is only one peaked gable: Sometimes it's a large one balanced by a smaller, flat-topped projection; in another case the gable is large and asymmetrical, and dominates the facade.

Reading drawings
When you're working with a professional on a complex renewal project, you can expect to see a variety of drawings, including the following.
• *Floor plans.* These are sometimes called *plan views.* They are two-dimensional, maplike renderings that show the arrangement of rooms, walls, windows, and doors on each floor.
• *Elevation drawings,* or *views,* provide a vertical representation of each side of the house,

RESTORATION

RENOVATION

from the foundation to the top of the roof.

• *Section drawings* are large-scale cutaway views of interior details that can't be seen from the outside.

• *Detail drawings* zero in on particular aspects of the job and usually lay out the precise way different materials are to be joined together.

• *Mechanical* and *electrical drawings* outline exactly how heating, plumbing, and electrical work will be done.

The total look

The goal of all these plans, of course, is to represent how your renewed home will look and live. With this in mind, consider how you might handle these key interior features.

• *Room shape.* Rooms in a restored house are likely to be smaller than those in a renovated dwelling, unless the home originally was built on a grand scale. Small rooms generally look better and seem more spacious if they're kept simple. They also may be less expensive to renew.

• *Doors and windows.* Repositioning an interior door to improve a room's layout is not difficult—once the opening is blocked up and a solid wall created, you'd never know the doorway had been there. Plan to leave window openings as they are, however; exterior walls are harder to rebuild.

• *Living centers.* A restoration will probably call for keeping living, dining, or other rooms as close to the original design as possible, although you can change the dimensions a bit for greater livability. Renovation designs, on the other hand, often call for tearing down interior walls or adding to the existing structure to create contemporary-style family centers. *(continued)*

THE DESIGN PROCESS
(continued)

Two specific rooms are most likely to cry out for attention in any house, whether it's a 1950s ranch awaiting its thirtieth-anniversary spruce-up or a dilapidated Victorian rambler in need of just about everything.

• *Kitchen.* The biggest deficiency in many kitchens is a poor arrangement of work centers. Plan for workable distances between the sink, stove, refrigerator, and associated counters. A three-cornered arrangement is almost always good; depending on the space you have and the way you like to work, consider U-shapes—good for large spaces—and peninsulas—good where you have ample floor space but not a lot of wall space. Islands, galleys, L's, and one-wall arrangements all have uses, too.

• *Bathroom(s).* Your home's plumbing system may limit what you can do, but in many old bathrooms, getting rid of an odd jog or bend in a wall can be a surprisingly effective way to open up space.

The plans on these two pages show that bath and kitchen placement or replacement is pivotal in either restoration or renovation. Paradoxically, the restoration process may sometimes involve more changes from the existing layout than would many approaches to renovation. Because the house featured in this chapter had been used as a two-family dwelling and had undergone modifications, restoring it meant undoing many of these changes.

The plans shown *at right* give you an idea of how different the restored house layout could be from the original—once-removed.

RESTORATION

RENOVATION

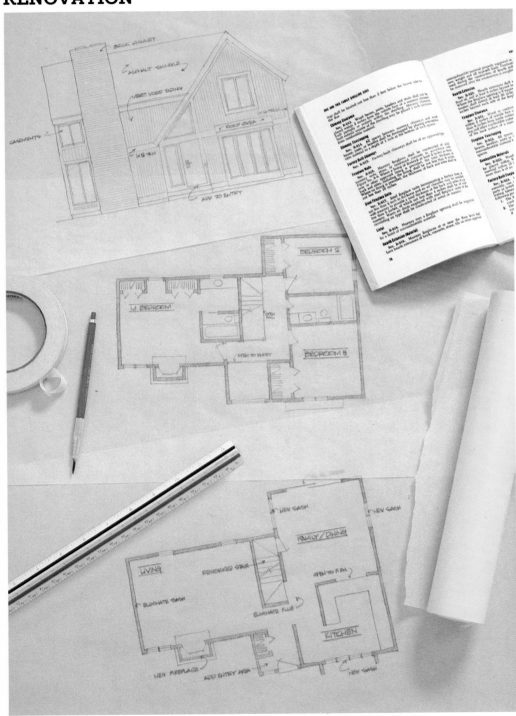

The kitchen has moved to the back room. On the upper floor, one set of stairs is to be removed and the bath relocated. The new master bath stays more or less in place, but with a different layout and access.

The main floor of the renovation, with tentative plans pictured *at left,* is somewhat closer to the two-family version. The kitchen stays in the same room as one of the earlier kitchens, but with a wall added to define a passageway from the entry hall to the family/dining room. The upstairs renovation plan reflects more changes—relocated baths and hallways, ample closet space, and a gallery overlooking the entry hall.

Outside

Your family's needs and tastes may be your primary concern, but also consider how your home's renewed exterior will relate to its surroundings. Any of several general approaches to exterior design will help a renovated house fit into the neighborhood.

- *Materials.* Try to use those that go well with the dominant type in the area, whether stucco, brick, or clapboard.
- *Texture.* Relate the texture of materials—rough or smooth brickwork, narrow or widely spaced clapboards, for example—to neighboring homes.
- *Colors.* Highly idiosyncratic colors or combinations make a personal statement, but they don't necessarily add up to effective design and may clash with the surroundings. If you want to do something different, be sure you do it well.
- *Details.* Relate important architectural details, such as door and window trim, cornices, and chimneys, to the neighborhood's predominant style and mood.

FINAL DESIGN CHOICES

As the two sets of plans shown here demonstrate, alternatives or additions to the original can often present appealing features that no one thought of the first time around. Evolutionary changes like these can be spurred by economics, aesthetics, or instinct.

Here, for example, restoration plans call for only one bath, rather than the two proposed on page 56. More attention—as well as some of the money saved by eliminating the second bath—is devoted to expanding main-floor living areas in a way compatible with the home's original appearance.

The renovation plans still call for two upstairs baths, but a third has been added to the main floor in a dramatic departure from the plans shown on page 57. This version maximizes main-floor living space and provides convenience for guests and family members.

Materials for restoration

Materials, textures, and colors help to establish the essential identity of any house. In a restoration where using the original materials is not practical, color and texture become especially important. Materials that you'd use in an old house restoration include the familiar standbys—stone, brick, clapboard, and, for the roof, slate, tile, or wood shingles. Where high cost or limited availability is a factor, substitutions such as asphalt roofing shingles may be acceptable.

Color is probably the most personal of design choices, so choose basic color schemes carefully. Ask your architect to draw a colored sketch showing you how the proposed scheme will look. Don't use a multitude of colors, unless they're highly appropriate to

RESTORATION

ELEVATION

UPPER LEVEL FLOOR PLAN

MAIN LEVEL FLOOR PLAN

roofing

paint scheme

portico brick

RENOVATION

ELEVATION

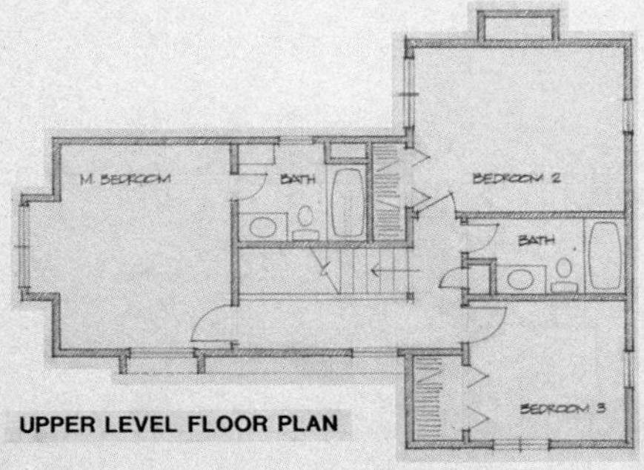

UPPER LEVEL FLOOR PLAN

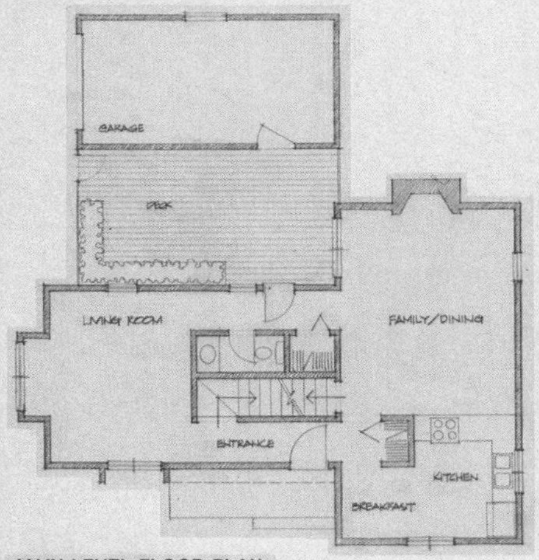

MAIN LEVEL FLOOR PLAN

roofing

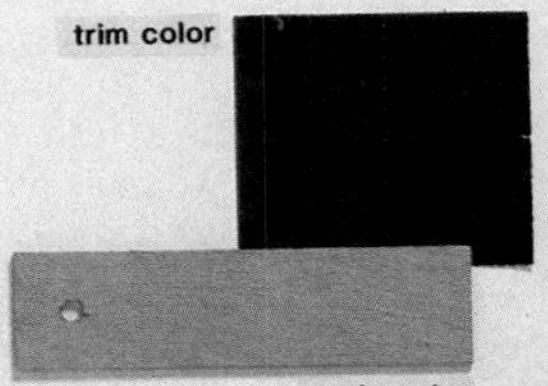

trim color

stain color

sash frames

door color

your home and neighborhood, and reserve bright hues for architectural focal points.

The deep brown asphalt shingles chosen for the roof of our restoration design (see the sample pictured *opposite*) are a practical and aesthetically appropriate alternative to the wood shingles used for the home's original roof. The warm earth tones selected for the restoration's exterior paint scheme are subtle and low key, but not bland, in keeping with the taste of the period in which the home was built.

The bricks specified for the floor of the new portico are, again, right for the style and period, although the way in which they are to be used is a new one, to be added in the interpretive rather than restorative spirit.

Materials for renovation

When renovation or modernization is the goal, many of the materials used for a restoration still may be appropriate. In many cases, the original materials will look the best, even when used in new ways. They are time-tested, attractive, and durable.

Modern materials such as vinyl or aluminum siding and metal window and door frames have a place in renovation projects, too. But shun obvious fakes such as artificial brick and stone.

The renovation plans *at left* show how close a new look can be to an old one. The plans call for board siding to be placed on the home's exterior and stained a pale earth tone, with darker brown trim. The metal window frames will be rich coppery brown, with silver-gray metal doors staying in the background. The roofing material chosen is the same as for the restoration.

(continued)

FINAL
DESIGN
CHOICES
(continued)

The final designs for the proposed restoration *above* and renovation *opposite* reflect many of the points discussed earlier in the chapter. Each is also a sensitive example of some additional principles of design that you may want to consider as you're developing your own renewal plans.

• Don't try to transform a building's interior just for the sake of change or novelty. What seems offbeat and intriguing at first may become inconvenient and unlivable when you're more familiar with it. As they do in the floor plans shown here, room designs should be opened up or closed down based on two things: research into the home's past and an honest appraisal of how your family will use the space.

• Don't change the basic structure of the house arbitrarily. In a restoration, you probably wouldn't want to anyway—to do so would be a contradiction in terms. Avoid the impulse in most cases, even if you're planning a thorough renovation. Even small and carefully designed additions, such as the bump-out on the left side of the renovation elevation

RESTORATION

upper level floor plan

master bedroom
bath
bedrm 2
bedrm 3

main level floor plan

carriage house
portico
kitchen
parlor
porch
dining room

RENOVATION

upper level floor plan

main level floor plan

shown here, should be made exceptions to the rule only if they fit into the rest of the house well, both inside and out.

Similarly, subtractions—the missing porch in the renovation is a good example—also require careful thought. Performing major structural surgery on an otherwise sound old house makes neither good aesthetic sense nor good economic sense.

• Think of the future as you plan. Make as few irrevocable changes as possible. Home-renewers-to-be may want at

least as good a chance to restore or renovate your house as you had.

• Avoid adding details from an earlier era to a house. This technique is mockingly called ''earlying up'' by veteran home renewers. Although the restoration elevation pictured *opposite* has a number of historical features that were absent from the house as photographed on page 47, they're all unquestionably from a time within the home's architectural life span.

NAILING DOWN COSTS

A s the figures on this and the opposite page so tellingly indicate, there's a price to be paid—and a large one, at that—for a whole-house restoration or renovation. As a general rule, however, purchasing a dilapidated dwelling for a low price and then restoring or renovating it makes better economic sense than buying a near-perfect home or building a comparable house from scratch. Quite simply, renewing costs less.

The tradeoff is measured another way—in time. Time spent waiting for the work to be done. Time spent doing some of the work yourself. Time spent dealing with inevitable discomfort, inconvenience, and frustration.

Begin with the essentials
As optimistic as the financial view may be for a well-chosen renewing project, you'll need to present detailed estimates of costs to lenders before they'll consider providing the funds you need. From the very beginning, keep an eye on the budget. It's often the first item to fall by the wayside when you're caught up in the enthusiasm of planning.

A good place to start is with the professional inspection that you had done before you bought the house. This provides a good early warning about structural or systemic improvements that *have* to be made, along with a rough estimate of the costs involved. Later, throughout the design stages, an experienced architect can offer reliable estimates for both labor and materials. Keep in mind, however, that architects may not always recommend the least costly possible solutions to design problems, and you may have to discuss more economical alternatives.

Overall costs will vary markedly, depending on the age and condition of the house, regional labor and material costs, the quality of products selected, and local contractors' requirements for overhead and profit. In addition, even a modest rate of inflation will instantly date published cost estimates.

Nevertheless, to give you an idea of the *kinds* of expenses you can expect to incur in a restoration or renovation, we took our two projects to a contractor and asked for estimated bids. The results appear in the boxes at right and opposite.

WHAT OUR RESTORATION MIGHT COST

The bids for doing our proposed restoration *at left* and proposed renovation *opposite* are general indicators of what you could expect to spend for a whole-house or large-scale home renewing project. In both cases, most of the largest sums cover roughly the same kinds of labor and materials: lumber, carpentry, plumbing, electrical upgrading, new heating and cooling systems, exterior trimwork, kitchen cabinets and appliances, and carpeting.

Some of the items listed in this box are more characteristic of a restoration than a renovation, however. These items include the special millwork, plastering, wrought-iron staves, and the exterior brickwork for both the portico and a period-style extension of the chimney.

Item	Bid
Building permit	$ 175
Lumber (rough)	3,120
Lumber (trim)	1,657
Shingles (labor and materials)	1,275
Framing (labor)	2,445

Exterior brick (materials)	280
Exterior brick (labor)	400
House plumbing	2,200
Electrical work	2,600
Appliance venting	65
Heating and air conditioning	1,775
Insulation	700
Drywall	1,920
Plastering	750
Special trim (materials)	1,675
Trim carpentry (labor)	3,700
Wrought iron	275
Special millwork	2,600
Gutters	260
Painting	1,100
Kitchen cabinets	875
Kitchen counters	260
Appliances	1,300
Hardware	75
Interior misc. (labor)	370
Exterior misc. (labor)	685
Trash hauling	250
Window cleanup	150
Light fixtures	1,300
Carpet	1,710
Hard-surface flooring	219
Sodding and lawn repair	500
Subtotal	$36,666
3% error allowance	1,100
20% overhead	7,556
Projected 25% profit	11,335
Total job price	$56,657

WHAT OUR RENOVATION MIGHT COST

Unlike a restoration, a renovation places few restrictions on what you can add to the home's original layout. If you need an extra bath, for example, the renovation approach permits you to fashion another in existing space.

Similarly, if you aren't satisfied with the home's total living area, you can put up an addition to boost square footage. A faithful restoration would make it much more difficult to work such changes into the plan.

Substantial changes of this kind are clearly visible at the bottom line, of course. Compare the costs listed in this box with those opposite. These include a new fireplace, new bathrooms, and an attached deck, all of which are absent from the restoration design and estimate. Together, they add more than $6,000 to the total bid.

Item	Bid
Building permit	$ 175
Masonry for new	
fireplace (labor)	830
(materials)	575
Fireplace	540
Chimney cap	
installation	75
Lumber (rough)	3,700
Lumber (trim)	2,200
Shingles (labor	
and materials)	1,275
Framing (labor)	2,800
Deck (labor)	350
Special labor (rough)	250
Plumbing	3,800
Electrical work	2,600
Heating and air	
conditioning	1,775
Appliance venting	35
Insulation	700
Drywall	2,175
Special trim items	895
Trim carpentry	4,200
Gutters	260
Painting	1,100
Casement windows	1,875
Kitchen cabinets	1,259
Bath vanities	375
Laminate	
counter tops	320
Marble counter tops	250
Wallpaper	700
Ceramic tile (labor	
and materials)	450
Appliances	1,300
Mirrors	75
Hardware	175
Shower doors	200
Interior misc.	
(labor)	370
Exterior misc.	
(labor)	200
Trash hauling	250
Window cleanup	150
Light fixtures	300
Carpet	1,275
Hard-surface	
flooring	519
Landscaping	350
Subtotal	$40,703
3% error allowance	1,221
20% overhead	8,384
Projected 25%	
profit	12,576
Total job price	$62,884

If you have a top-of-the-line design but a bottom-of-the-barrel budget, don't automatically scale down or cut back on your plans. Consider three methods to get what you're looking for.

• Do part of the work yourself, to cut down on labor costs. Some jobs (see page 65) are well within the range of an average do-it-yourselfer. Do make sure, however, that you really can do what you think you can, or today's savings may have to be applied to tomorrow's or next year's repair bills. Be sure, too, that you have both the time and the energy to devote to the project, and that you're willing to put up with the accompanying mess longer than if it were being done by professionals.

• Compromise a little on materials. The difference in price between what's best and what's good can be considerable, but the difference in appearance and serviceability may be much smaller. Choosing from odd lots or discontinued lines is another money-saving maneuver. But don't go overboard and buy the least expensive materials and items on the market. You may have to replace them sooner than you expect, and your initial savings will go out the door with them.

• Complete the work in stages, paying for each as you can afford it. Begin by remedying clearcut hazards; go on to weatherproofing the house and curing any structural problems; finally, turn to interior projects such as redoing the kitchen and baths, restoring architectural details, redecorating living areas, and so forth. Staging the work calls for extra patience, of course, since it may be a year or much more before you see the final results of your efforts.

And don't forget to . . .
As you plan, include expenses that aren't technically part of the construction budget but have to be accounted for anyway. These include:
• Fees for the professional assistance of a home inspector, architect, and any other experts, such as an attorney.
• Costs for new furniture and household accessories.
• Costs for municipal services that need to be tied into the renewed home.
• A contingency fund of between 10 and 15 percent of the total construction costs to cover unforeseen problems.

GETTING
THE WORK
DONE

When you're contemplating a whole-house renewal, expert help at the planning stage is usually a good investment. Sound advice at this point will not only make it much more likely that you'll get just what you're after, it may even keep you from wasting money on unnecessarily expensive labor and materials.

Who can help? For a major restoration or renovation, an experienced architect who understands the entire process is probably the best choice. The key is to come up with someone who is interested in residential design and has experience in renewing old houses. To find a qualified professional, talk to people you know who have had similar work done in the recent past; then inspect the results for yourself. If no one you know can recommend someone, check with local lending institutions, real estate agents, building inspectors, and professional societies.

An architect can provide a full menu of services from which you can choose any one or a combination, depending on how much help you need or can afford. The services include: focusing tentative proposals, preparing rough sketches and plans of the existing house, developing final drawings for a contractor or subcontractors, and supervising construction to ensure that it follows the plans and meets all legal requirements.

For limited advice, you'll usually be billed at an hourly rate, but for full-service assignments, many architects charge a percentage (10-15 percent) of actual or estimated construction costs, plus expenses. Some architects, however, will

work for an hourly fee throughout, again plus expenses, with the total bill not to exceed an agreed-upon maximum. This may be the best option for you, since it helps avoid disagreements about budget overruns.

Calling all contractors

Many home renewers hire a general contractor to do all or most of the work. It's crucial that you find one whose work is superior and whose integrity is well established. Equally important, you'll need an individual with experience at doing the kind of work you have in mind.

Although an architect will be able to make recommendations, it may pay for you to do some digging on your own. Again, ask for names and references from sources such as those discussed above. Ask the questions that matter most.
• Is the quality of the contractor's work uniformly high?
• Does he keep to schedules?
• Is he dependable, willing to consider well-intentioned suggestions, easy to get along with?
• Does he work with an eye on the budget?

Keep searching until you have four or five likely prospects; then sit down with each to discuss the outlines of the job. There's no need yet to unveil finished plans or request formal bids. Ask to see for yourself similar work the contractor has done. Use these interviews not only to assess the quality of the contractor's work, but also to gauge the nature of his personality. If any candidate is gruff, overbearing, uncommunicative, or, by contrast, unreasonably optimistic, cross him off your list.

For this kind of project, any contractor you're considering must be bonded, insured, and covered by workmen's compensation. If a contractor doesn't have proper coverage, you may be financially responsible for injuries suffered on the job.

Finally, check bank references, the local Better Business Bureau, and consumer protection agencies to find out if anyone has registered complaints about the contractors on your list.

Out for bids

Once you've narrowed your choices down to three, it's time to request detailed bids in writing. All bids must be comparable; to make sure they are, be careful about submitting exactly the same plans and specifications to each bidder. There's no room for error at this point, so it's up to you and your architect to confirm that everyone is using the same facts and figures.

Deciding which bid to accept isn't always easy. If all three are fairly close, other things being equal, taking the lowest one is usually the best choice. Beware, however, of a bid that is substantially below the other two—the contractor may have neglected to include a major part of the job, or he may be underbidding on purpose to get the business. Both reasons signal stormy times ahead: inferior workmanship and materials, or requests for more money later.

Although you will probably be inclined to discard an extremely high bid, don't automatically reject one that is a little higher than the others. If the contractor's reputation and personality are clearly a cut above the others, go ahead and choose him.

Signing up

A contract will seal the deal. It should include a starting date, detailed specifications, a guarantee for at least three years, and a completion date. Don't let this last point slip by, or you may find yourself at the mercy of a too-busy contractor who's buying time at your expense. To forestall lengthy delays, include the phrase "time is of the essence." This is a neat legal way of saying that you are serious about getting the job done on schedule.

Similarly, insert a phrase requiring the contractor to proceed with all parts of the job "in a workmanlike manner." This means the work is to be done correctly. Insist that any contractor you hire sign a waiver of liens before the subcontractors arrive.

The contract also will lay out a schedule of payments. Don't agree to put down hefty sums up front. These mainly improve the contractor's cash flow, again at your expense. A common, generally accepted formula calls for a third of the money to be paid when you sign, a second third when the project is about halfway done, and a final third when it is completed. Consider including language that allows you to withhold 10 percent or more of the last payment for 30 to 60 days after the work is done. During that time, the work will be put to the test of real-life use; if necessary, you can wield the power of the last payment to get corrections made.

Treat the contract as a living document. If you do want something done differently—although at this stage it shouldn't be too different—just put the new deal in writing, along with its cost, before the change is made by the workers.

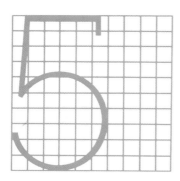

WHAT OTHERS HAVE DONE: NINE CASE STUDIES

There's nothing like someone else's successful renewal project to make you feel confident about the prospects for your own. If others have worked miracles of creativity and commitment, you can, too. The not-so-secret keys to successful renewing: Have the right attitude and know what to expect. Your house will be torn up, messy, and inconvenient while the work is going on, but you must hold on to your vision of what the end result has been for others—and will be for you.

Small, dark, 1930s houses are no strangers to anyone with an interest in older homes. When the present owners bought the home pictured here, the interior was dim and the rooms were confining. Imaginative remodeling, however, changed all that—and without altering the home's overall dimensions.

Originally, the house was a one-level, three-bedroom structure with an unfinished attic. The owners wanted to open up the main level and put the attic to work as primary living space. They also needed to tighten up the house for greater energy efficiency.

Downstairs, the family replaced a pair of double-hung windows with French doors, creating the light, airy, and spacious living room pictured *at right*. These doors open to a new brick-paved courtyard, sheltered by the stuccoed-block wall visible in the inset photo. Upstairs, the attic was transformed into a new master bedroom and bath.

To provide sufficient headroom in the new upstairs bedroom, the living room ceiling had to be lowered slightly. To compensate for this, new beams were left visible and the lowered ceiling was installed above rather than below them. With the ceiling, beams, wall, fireplace, and trim all painted white, you scarcely notice that the room is a few inches less than standard height.

Another pair of French doors (not shown) leads into the living room from a vestibule, which was once a screened porch. Closed, the doors turn the vestibule into an air-lock entry; open, they're a gateway to additional living space.

ADDING ON

The grandly scaled turn-of-the-century home shown here had not deteriorated, but it did need a "space-lift." Renewing it didn't mean replacing old, worn-out parts, but rather, adding sparkling new ones. When the owners decided to add a study and a new living room, they had two main concerns: to retain the character of the old house outside and to suit their contemporary life-style inside. In other words, their challenge was to blend the nineteenth and twentieth centuries within one structure.

The original front porch seemed a natural place to swing out and around with a curved addition—the new study. This circular sweep at one end of the porch, shown *below,* harks back to the Victorian era. To keep the addition from looking like an afterthought, its new double-glazed windows were carefully placed and sized for compatibility with existing windows.

To minimize upkeep, the owners used aluminum siding on the addition; the rest of the house had been re-sided with aluminum a decade earlier.

A step in time

Although the house's street-side appearance maintains its original character, the back of the house is a different story. Here a decidedly twentieth-century addition (exterior not shown) angles out into the yard, creating the dramatically contemporary living room shown *at right.*

A new steel I-beam replaces the rear wall to support the house's upper stories. The beam allows for open space between the new and old structures, making it possible to use lots of glass on the nonbearing, south-facing exterior walls.

The new living area is a few steps lower than the floor level of the existing house. This difference focuses attention both on the upper windows and the lush foliage immediately beyond them. A sculpted fireplace wall serves as a conventional focal point in unconventional dress. The curving free-form shelf and niches beside the fireplace are new; they're examples of innovative applications of traditional plastering techniques.

RE-CREATING THE PAST

This 1880s house, part of a neighborhood renovation project (see pages 82 and 83), had been saved from the wrecking ball and given a second chance before the present owner purchased it. Antiquated heating, plumbing, and electrical systems had been replaced and the exterior, pictured *opposite,* had been carefully restored with an eye to authentic detail. The house was not only livable, it retained much of its nineteenth-century character.

But inside, authenticity had occasionally taken second place to the builder's convenience. Walls and ceilings gleamed with decidedly non-Victorian white paint, and wall-to-wall carpet covered the floors. The new owner, devotee of Victoriana, began renewing again to restore a nineteenth-century atmosphere inside as well as out.

The carpets were the first to go. Underneath was the beautiful strip-oak flooring of the original house, a perfect background for handsome Oriental rugs used in the living room and in the dining room pictured *at right.*

The interior woodwork had already been restored, so the owner next gave the walls touches of Victorian charm. In some rooms she stenciled designs on painted walls, a treatment popular during the Victorian era. Other rooms, such as the dining room, were papered with patterns appropriate to the house in design, scale, and coloring.

If you're planning wall treatments for a home of Victorian vintage, here are some points to keep in mind.
• Victorian walls almost always had a border capping the wall treatment.

• Dadoes of natural wood, used with wallpaper, were popular during the late nineteenth and early twentieth centuries.
• Most reproduction papers of pre-1850 patterns are copies of expensive wall coverings that only wealthy householders could afford. If your home is a relative modest one whose original owners probably couldn't have purchased papers of this type, these wall coverings may not be appropriate for the home now, either. For more about choosing appropriate surface treatments for restored homes, see Chapter 9—''Keeping Up Appearances''—and Chapter 10—''Finishing and Furnishing.''

CHANGING OLD HOUSES

If you're concerned about historical accuracy in your renewing efforts, here are some guidelines.
• Don't destroy the home's architectural character when you bring it up to modern functional standards.
• Preserve distinguishing qualities by minimizing removal or alteration of historical or architectural features.
• Repair rather than replace deteriorated features. If features must be replaced, they should duplicate the original.
• Make additions in such a way that if in the future they are removed, the essential form and integrity of the structure won't be compromised.
• Don't falsify the past by trying to make the building look like an authentic example of earlier or later architecture.

To learn more about these considerations, turn to page 48.

MAKING A PLAIN HOUSE PRETTY

Some houses are just bursting with obvious potential for renewing. With others, the rewards are not so obvious.

The small, drab house in the photo *at upper right* was tucked into a narrow corner lot and offered only 800 square feet of living space. Many prospective buyers passed it by, despite its low price. But the new owners saw its possibilities. They envisioned it as an attractive cottage with bright and imaginative interior spaces that would highlight their vintage furnishings.

The first step in renewing was to raise the attic roof on the front and rear of the house, creating the extra gable visible *at lower right*. This made room for a study, second bedroom, and bath upstairs.

Next, the exterior was restored to its original charm. The front porch was rebuilt; redwood siding was stained a soft gray. The gingerbread trim, which had been removed and stored by a previous owner, was put back on the porch. This trim also served as a design base for new trim, which was added to the gables.

Inside, the owners removed the living room ceiling, creating a more spacious feeling. A new stairway, shown *opposite*, not only defines living and dining areas, but provides a dramatic focal point as well.

White walls and ceilings throughout diffuse light evenly on both levels, and the open plan allows air as well as people to circulate freely.

In this case, a good location justified major reconstruction of a dowdy house. In other instances, an appealing house could be in a poor location. If so, you might be wise to purchase the house and move it to a new address, as discussed in the box at right.

MOVING A HOUSE

When you look at anything as solid and seemingly fixed as a house, it's hard to imagine that it could even budge. Yet within days, movers can jack even a masonry-veneered structure off its foundation, slide the house onto a truck, and cart it to a new site.

Just about any house *can* be moved, but there's lots to think about before you do anything so drastic as taking a house off its foundation.
- *Structural soundness.* Minor deterioration won't affect a home's movability, but a rotted sill, excessive settlement, or other serious problems will. (More about these on pages 40-43.)
- *Movers.* Use only reputable and knowledgeable professionals—the stakes are high. Ask for references and talk to owners of structures the firm has moved.
- *Cost.* The movers will further analyze the home's structural soundness, survey the route it must travel, and evaluate what a move will cost. It may be prohibitively expensive.
- *Utilities.* Utility companies charge for any help with low-hanging power and telephone lines.
- *Red tape.* You may need a permit for the move and may encounter rules regarding the streets along which the house will be moved.

BEFORE

AFTER

REVIVING A ROW HOUSE

Transforming a century-old row house into an up-to-the-minute dwelling is a big job. And if you're doing the contracting and much of the labor yourself, the job is even bigger. That kind of responsibility and achievement was exactly what the owners of the shingled house shown here wanted. Their project took five years and thousands of do-it-yourself working hours, but the owners are the first to say it was well worth it.

To accomplish a major, down-to-the-studs remodeling, the homeowners played a variety of roles—everything from general contractor to journeyman to laborer.

The space changes inside the old house created an entirely new environment—one well suited to an active young couple's life-style. If you study the "before" and "after" plans *at lower right,* you'll see that the confining wall between the entry and the living room was removed, eliminating the closed-in tunnel effect of the original Victorian living room.

An old lavatory at the back of the house was removed and its space incorporated into the newly remodeled kitchen.

Even though much of the home's original interior trim was replaced or removed, the old crown moldings and ceiling beams were retained in the living room, pictured *at upper right.* Painted white to match the walls, they offer subtle detailing, without closing the room in, as dark wood or contrasting colors might.

Upstairs, the middle bedroom was transformed into a bath/dressing area. The new walls were painted white and the new Douglas fir trim was finished in mellow natural tones. The owners devoted lots of time and effort to stripping down the old painted

stairway to bare wood and finishing it in the same golden tones as the new upstairs trim.

The home's exterior, shown *opposite,* remains handsome and understated, with natural wood shingles and dramatic black trim. Thanks to contrasting bottoms-up shades used throughout the house, even the time-mellowed exterior achieves a crisp new look.

Though this one is entirely owner-occupied, many row houses lend themselves to up-and-down duplexing, offering an opportunity to include a rental unit that can help pay the mortgage. Developing a renewed house into an income-producing property also can offer substantial tax breaks, as explained on opposite page.

BEFORE

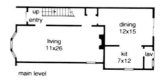

AFTER

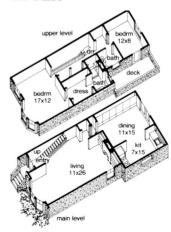

TAX INCENTIVES FOR RENTAL PROPERTIES

The Economic Recovery Tax Act of 1981 offers several preservation tax incentives. If you're rehabilitating a historic income-producing building, whether it's residential, commercial, or industrial, you can claim a 25 percent investment tax credit for rehabilitating the *income-producing* part of the structure.

The building cannot be used solely as a private residence: If you occupy all floors yourself, it's not eligible; if you occupy two and rent out the other two as apartments, it may be eligible if other conditions are met.

The building must be subject to depreciation as the Internal Revenue Code defines it. In addition, the Secretary of the Interior must certify that your building is historic and that the rehabilitation is appropriate to the character of the building or district.

In addition to federal tax incentives, some states and municipalities offer tax incentives for preserving and rehabilitating historic buildings. Check with your local or state historic preservation office, accountant, or tax attorney for more information.

MAKING LESS FROM MORE

ouses are anything but static. Their uses change, expand, even double up, all at the coaxing of their owners. The 1914 house pictured here had been many things to many people. It started out as a single-family dwelling, but with the housing shortage following World War II, it was converted to a two-family, side-by-side residence. Now it's once again a one-family home.

The new owner, together with some handy friends, put in new heating, wiring, plumbing, insulation, double-glazed windows, and drywall. More important, he revised the floor plan so that two compact apartments became a single dramatic house with plenty of natural light and not an inch of wasted space.

Redesigning the space started with ripping out one living room ceiling to incorporate the previously unused attic into a two-story-high living room. The new vaulted ceiling follows the original roofline, but it's a foot or so below the roof decking, leaving ample room for insulation. (The other living room became a well-proportioned bedroom; see floor plans *at right.)* The old entry gave way to a larger entry that accommodates the stairway to the new second-floor loft.

To create the spacious, airy room pictured *at right,* the wall dividing the entry and living room was opened up with two cutouts. One provides a large accessway to the living room; the other, a slice at the top, makes a "railing" wall for the bedroom/study in the loft.

Old double-hung windows in this portion of the house were replaced by a series of skylights that bathe both levels in natural light. The fireplace wall was redesigned to be the focal point of the room.

BEFORE　　　　　**AFTER**

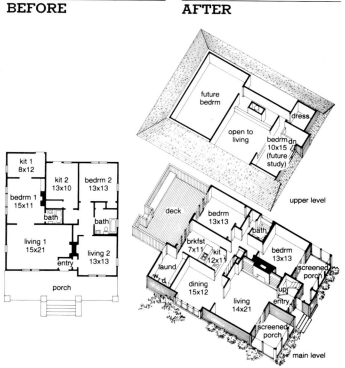

CONVERTING
A SHOP
INTO A HOME

After almost three centuries as a business establishment (it had been a bakery, an ice cream parlor, and an antique shop), this compact, two-story, 20x30-foot brick building became a home for the present owners. Time and use had taken their toll, and recycling this property took great faith as well as creativity and hard work.

The exterior, shown *below,* was left mostly intact, the way it looked in its most recent business phase. It's in the interior that you really see the deft touch of the present homeowners. The first floor is an open-plan combination of foyer, library, living, dining, and kitchen areas, with different functions set off from each other by furniture arrangements rather than by walls. (Upstairs, a bath and two bedrooms provide privacy and comfort for the owners and overnight guests.)

The cozy charm of the portion of the first floor pictured *at left* demonstrates the success of this conversion. Antique blue and white plates highlight the dining area, contrasting gently with the pink and white theme of the living area.

CONVERTING BUILDINGS

There's less red tape involved in converting a commercial building into a residence than you might expect—certainly less than fitting a business into a private home. But to avoid unnecessary steps or the need to do something over to meet standards, check with local authorities *before* you begin any conversion project.
• To convert to a single-family dwelling, you must deal with a building inspector, who will make sure that the heating system, electric and plumbing lines, and exits meet building codes for private residences.
• To convert from a commercial to a rental residential property, you also must deal with the local government agency in charge of inspecting for health hazards.

BRINGING
NEW LIFE TO AN
OLD FARM

When property has been in a family for years, it's easy to overlook its potential. When the property in question is a 50-acre farm that includes the site of a burned-out summer home, several outbuildings, and a granary built in 1847, it's a challenge to define just what the potential is.

At one time, the owners of this Maryland homestead lived in a contemporary house on the acreage. In their spare time, they converted the dilapidated outbuildings into rental properties. When it came time to do something with the old granary, however, the family decided to transform it into their year-round home.

For three years, family members devoted weekends and evenings to turning the weathered old building into the gracious home pictured *above*. All the materials used in the project either were from the original structure or were otherwise appropriate to the architecture and the period.

The home's exterior was faced with native rose-tone brick. An authentic catslide, or saltbox, roof caps the exterior, and brick steps ascend to the massive entry.

Adding on

The colonial-style "keeping room" shown *opposite* was added to the original granary. Here, too, materials and furnishings carry on the spirit of the renovation. Bricks that were fired on the farm serve as facing for the wall-to-wall fireplace, and more bricks pave the floor. Horizontal paneling over the fireplace and beneath the dado started out as the granary's original exterior siding. The ceiling beams are rough-sawn hemlock, hewn from a nearby tree that was felled during a windstorm.

Mellow, country-style appointments furnish the keeping room. A drop-leaf table and a pair of armless Windsor chairs occupy center stage. Comfortable upholstered chairs face the hearth. Rustic implements, used as accessories, remind family members of the farm's working past.

Finding renovating
materials

If you're renovating a vintage home and don't have a farm to recycle, here's information that can make your search for appropriate materials a little easier.

• To match old wood, choose new wood with a similar appearance, even if it's from a

different kind of tree. Over the years, the characteristic properties of wood can change. Colors may darken or bleach out. Grains may open or tighten up. This means that matching the woods of the same species and achieving the same appearance, despite a difference in age, is difficult.

• If you're replacing lumber in an old house, remember that lumber dimensions have changed. In older homes, a 2x4 really measured 2x4 inches; today's 2x4 is 1½x3½ inches and other sizes are similarly smaller. If you're replacing a structural member, it may be necessary to have it custom-milled.

• Clean old bricks before reusing them. Soak them in water overnight, then brush them with a natural-bristle brush. Don't use a wire brush on old bricks—the wire may damage their soft surfaces.

• Salvage materials from old houses on the brink of demolition can include nearly anything you need for a renovation, but be a careful buyer—some salvage items cost more than custom-made reproductions. Others may need so much work to bring them back to usable condition that the effort just isn't worth-

while. If you do want to use salvage materials, you'll be better off dealing directly with a demolition firm rather than buying from an architectural salvage retailer. Retailers offer a good selection of materials, but charge high prices to cover overhead.

To learn more about locating specialized parts for a renovation or restoration, see Chapter 9—"Keeping Up Appearances."

HOW TO MOTHBALL AN OLD HOUSE

Protecting an uninhabited structure until you're ready to start work is sometimes referred to as "mothballing." Vacant houses are not as stable as buildings that are lived in, and some deterioration is inevitable, but you can take measures to protect an empty house from serious damage.

• Shut off all electricity to reduce the possibility of fire resulting from frayed wiring or malfunctioning appliances.

• Inspect roofs and make sure drainage systems are functioning. Leaks and flooding can ruin walls and ceilings and eventually rot away structural members.

• Remove all trash from both the house and the yard. Besides reducing fire hazards, a tidy appearance tells the world that someone cares about the property.

• Secure doors and windows so animals and unauthorized persons can't get in.

• Provide heat in winter if possible; if not, provide outside ventilation for each room, especially the attic, basement, and crawl spaces. This minimizes moisture buildup.

• Inspect your house periodically so any problems can be taken care of as soon as possible.

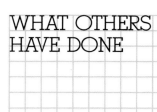

RENEWING
AN ENTIRE
NEIGHBORHOOD

Wonderful things happen to neighborhoods when people care about them. The tidy row of nineteenth-century homes shown *at left* is an example of a street that came back to life after decades of deterioration.

This is Milwaukee Avenue, situated on the outskirts of Minneapolis in the 1880s—and now conveniently close to the center-city of the 1980s. The houses were built to copybook plans on space-conserving half-lots. They were the first planned workers' community in the area and were originally inhabited by immigrants who came to work in the rail yards.

About 90 years after construction, Milwaukee Avenue was declared to have outlived its usefulness, and authorities scheduled it for demolition. The threat of demolition provided a rallying point for the neighborhood, however, and a committee was formed to initiate rehabilitation efforts.

In 1974, the avenue was placed on the National Register of Historic Places; after that, the Minneapolis Metropolitan Housing Corporation stepped in, bought several houses, and began renovation.

The homes had been built without basements on limestone foundations that had begun to crumble, so new underpinnings were a priority. The homes were jacked up, basements were dug, and new foundations were constructed.

Great care was taken to restore the exteriors to their original appearance. Used bricks from other old buildings were recycled for repairs where necessary. The gingerbread trim from one of the street's houses, which had held on to its original porch, was used as the pattern for replacement trim on the other houses.

COULD YOUR COMMUNITY QUALIFY FOR BLOCK GRANTS?

If your neighborhood is 50 years old, or older, and most of its homes were built in the same era, it may qualify for block grants that will ease the renovation or rehabilitation process. Here are some things to think about and steps to take to make your neighborhood renovation work go more smoothly.

● You don't have to form a neighborhood association, but it may help allocate responsibilities if there's a formal organization behind you.

● To qualify for a federal rehabilitation grant, properties must be listed on the National Register of Historic Places. Check with your state historic preservation agency for information about how to file a federal grant application. If a neighborhood group is interested in applying for a listing, it may be entitled to special grants for surveying and planning.

● All restoration must be historically accurate and completed within a given period.

● Usually government restoration grants must be matched dollar for dollar by private money.

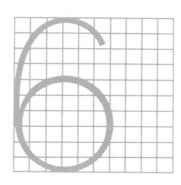

RENEWING
EXTERIORS

A neglected old house
is a wasted resource—a
potential treasure put aside.
Reviving a shabby exterior
could amount to nothing
more than applying a fresh
coat of paint; or it could be
as arduous as stripping
away old asphalt siding
and restoring the nine-
teenth-century clapboards
underneath. You may
choose to remove an addi-
tion that should never have
been added or replace gingerbread that should never
have been removed. The
following pages present a
dozen old houses with
fresh faces.

FAITHFUL
RESTORATION

Although some rooms required extensive reno-vation, the exterior of the farmhouse pictured *at right* looks much as it did when the home was built in the 1870s, right down to the rain barrels.

Originally the showplace of a prosperous farm, the house had suffered decades of twentieth-century neglect. Its wiring and plumbing were anti-quated and in poor condition, and much of the outside woodwork had decayed after years of exposure to harsh Wisconsin winters. The basic structure of the house, however, was sound.

Though there had been few repairs in recent years, there also had been few changes and no out-of-period additions or "improvements." The basics of the original 1870s exterior were there, just wait-ing to be restored.

Restoration in this case meant putting lots of pieces back together. Sagging porch-es were jacked up and rebuilt; then replacements for missing columns, balusters, and rails were custom-milled.

Because the house had been vacant for a time, many windows were broken. These were reglazed and their rotted frames reconstructed with new lumber. New wood storm win-dows, tightly weather-stripped, button up the house against winter's worst.

The owners replaced damaged siding with identical shiplapped boards, then paint-ed everything a soft gray, accented by white trim. A new roof of weathered-gray wood shingles tops off this good-as-new old house.

(continued)

FAITHFUL RESTORATION
(continued)

If you're aiming to restore your home's exterior to its original state, the more documentation you can find, the better. Old photos, prints, or paintings from the local library or historical society and recollections of longtime local residents can help you authenticate how your house looked when it was built. (For more about researching a restoration, see page 43.)

If, however, you favor *interpretive restoration*—incorporating stylistic elements of the period without exactly re-creating the past—you have a little more leeway. A solid knowledge of the architecture of the period and the region will help, and may be the best you can do if your house is not documented. Using an interpretive approach, you can fill in the details with what *might* have been. In other words, with interpretive restoration, you can style an exterior that's faithful to the past without precisely duplicating it.

Color is a key
Giving an old house a fresh coat of paint isn't all there is to a successful restoration, although it's certainly a vital aspect of the job. The color of the new paint is as important as the quality of the finish.

For example, if you're bringing an 80-year-old Queen Anne house back to decorative life, you may, through painstaking scraping, find out that it was originally painted dark red with dark green trim and gold accents. If scrupulous restoration is your goal, then these are the colors you'd choose to repaint with. But if interpretive restoration is what you have in mind, all you really need to know is the *kind* of color scheme used for Queen Anne houses. As you may already know, they were not painted

white; dark tones—usually several of them—prevailed. This means that you could repaint your house with other earth tones and still be historically correct.

The wrought-iron fence surrounding the compact Victorian house shown *opposite* contributes old-fashioned charm to the restoration. But without its carefully selected color scheme, the house would lose much of its distinction. Here, mustard-color siding is appropriate to the home's style. White paint highlights the ornate window frames and

draws attention to the fence. Bold, darker swaths of paint define the rooflines and window tops.

Architectural changes
In terms of color, the dark red shingles and two-tone gray trim of the rambling house shown *above* are close to the historic originals. Architecturally, however, this house reflects something of a departure from its past.

The original front porch had been destroyed by a storm-felled tree. In replacing it, the owners built a larger porch that includes a gabled gazebo. Besides providing an outdoor dining room adjacent to the one indoors, the gazebo helps downplay an awkward, out-of-

period addition built by earlier owners.

If you're wondering if your house has the same shape now that it did originally, look for clues both on its exterior and on similar homes. For example, if there's the ghost of a shed's roofline on the back of your colonial farmhouse, or if other homes built at the same time yours was typically have pediments over the entries, you may want to consider restoring these features.

A RENOVATION THAT RAISED THE ROOF

BEFORE

AFTER

Restoration aims to conserve a home's architecture. Renovation can be an exercise in creative problem solving. Sometimes renovation calls upon solutions that weren't available at the time of original construction, and sometimes it solves problems that didn't exist or weren't perceived when the house was first built.

The triple-peaked bungalow shown *above* was perfectly adequate in its day, but it had begun to look drab and dated by the 1980s. Previous owners had tried to modernize its appearance with an angled entry deck and other small touches, but the current owners felt something on a more dramatic scale was needed.

Their decision: to add a shed-roofed entry and totally face-lift the exterior. The result, pictured *at right,* amounts to a new, contemporary-style home at the same address.

The new entry was made by extending the roof of the original front-most gable to the height of the main roof peak. A pair of supporting fins under the roof extension provides vertical accents balanced by boxing around the porch. For maximum sturdiness, the fins

rest on concrete piers camouflaged by nonbearing shingled extension walls.

To tie everything together, the bungalow's original lap siding was replaced with cedar shingles that were stained a soft, elegant gray.

A word to the energy-wise

Removing the siding offered an important opportunity to bring the home up to contemporary standards of comfort and energy efficiency. After the siding was stripped off, the owners had cellulose insulation blown into the wall cavities.

Although window openings remain the same, the windows themselves were replaced with tight, new, triple-glazed units.

Examine the roof's left slope, and you can find evidence of one other heat-conserving change—a new, prefabricated fireplace. Boxing in the fireplace's chimney brings yet another sculptural element to a bold new exterior.

A transformation as dramatic as this one doesn't come cheap, but a major renovation often costs far less than either new construction or buying another home.

A RENOVATED
RANCH HOUSE

A house needn't be older than you are to be renovated. Not all houses are born beautiful, and others fade quickly after construction. If the style of a house is dated or the detailing is unattractive or insufficient, new architectural details can perk it up. If the problem is more substantial, major renovation can lead to improvements inside as well as out.

The long, lean contemporary shown here originated as a compact 1950s ranch with a bland exterior. By the time the present owners bought it, the house was in need of new siding. A re-siding job, coupled with several new decks and minor structural and landscaping changes, led to a major transformation.

The new rough-sawn plywood siding, installed over the original siding and interspersed with battens, gives the entire exterior a custom-built look. Pared-down and carefully selected landscaping materials add the finishing touches.

Only one aspect of the makeover directly affected interior spaces: Two bump-outs, each 2 feet deep, enlarged the front bedrooms. Inside, the bump-outs add enough square footage to allow for extra closets and study space. Their exterior walls, now flush with the deep roof overhang, flank the main front windows, adding visual interest to the front exterior shown *at left*. New flowering plants and shrubbery fill a recess between the bump-outs.

Three new decks—two in back (shown *below*) and one in front—add to the home's visual appeal and its outdoor living space. The front deck, visible toward the right in the photo *at left*, leads visitors graciously and efficiently from a parking area to the front door. Low walls at the edges of the decks provide privacy, and new border plantings bring distinction to the setting.

PAINT:
COLOR AND
CONTRAST

The purely practical function of paint is to protect a home's exterior structure from wear and tear. But paint—or, more precisely, color—is also an extension of the architecture itself, helping to delineate and define style, line, and form.

Colors of the past

Historically, color preferences have changed along with architectural styles. Colonial homes, for example, typically displayed sharp contrasts between body and trim colors in order to highlight such features as window and door detailing, shutters, and cupolas. Homes of the late eighteenth and early nineteenth centuries were often painted in subdued tones of gray, tan, blue, and brown to harmonize with natural surroundings. White was popular too, especially for Greek Revival homes.

Early Victorians preferred delicate hues—grays, pinks, tans, and yellows. Later Victorians initiated the use of rich color schemes such as those discussed on page 87. Dark colors were commonly used for the body of the house, with brighter contrasting tones accenting the trim. These relatively complex combinations complemented the increasingly ornate architecture of the middle and late nineteenth century. By the late Victorian era, buildings in such styles as Queen Anne, Shingle, Stick, and Eastlake tended toward an even darker palette of browns, oranges, olives, and reds.

As more compact homes such as bungalows became popular around the turn of the century, the subtle shades of the early Victorian era returned to favor. As Colonial Revival designs swept the country in the early 1900s, house colors

became even lighter, going back to pastels and to white.

Practical matters

There's more to color selection than knowing the date your home was built and the colors used at that time. Climate, location, and even landscaping are factors, too. For example, lighter colors have always been popular in the Southwest, where light-colored exterior walls reflect the hot sun and help keep homes' interiors cool. Dark colors, on the other hand, absorb light and can help raise indoor temperatures. In cities, where pollution is a fact of life, beige might replace white, and darker trim tones take the place of easily smudged brights.

The deep red paint on the farmhouse *above* suits the cool climate in which the house is located, as well as

the angular gabled style of the building. The pastel tones of the dainty but unshaded southern Victorian *opposite* help moderate the home's interior temperature during summer days, when it is exposed to the heat of the sun for much of the afternoon.

Color basics

Different colors create dramatically different effects, depending on how they reflect or absorb light. Use colors to accent attractive features of a house and downplay awkward ones. For example, paint a small house a light color if you want it to look larger, and choose a dark color for a large house if you'd like it to look less massive. You can perk up a bland house with a contrast between body and trim colors; if proportions seem wrong, try tone-on-tone combinations—

for example, light blue paint on the lower half of a tall house and darker blue above will make the structure seem more compact.

Depending on your home's style, you may have an abundance of interesting trim to accentuate. Trim includes the fascia, shutters, casings, windows, doors, dormers, chimneys, gutters, and downspouts. The last two items, however, rarely boast any architectural significance.

Some dormers offer distinctive shapes and great possibilities for creative painting. (See page 97 for an example of a finely detailed mansard dormer.) If your dormers are not attractive, painting them the same color as the part of the house they adjoin—either the body of the house or the roof—will minimize their impact. *(continued)*

PAINT:
COLOR AND
CONTRAST
(continued)

As much as anything, color is a matter of personal preference. No matter how historically correct a color is, don't use it if you don't like it. Develop a sense of what colors and combinations you like, then use the basic aesthetic principles discussed on the preceding pages to help you decide how to bring out the best of your home, whether it's Carpenter Gothic, Colonial, or mysteriously eclectic.

Colorful case studies

The warm-toned beige clapboards on the Cape Cod Colonial pictured *at upper right* set the stage for an original and very successful tricolor paint scheme. You might expect to see a house like this painted white with green or black shutters and a red door, but the owners of this home wanted a more subdued effect. After deciding on the beige body color, they chose a light eggshell hue to highlight the windows and the charmingly detailed front door frame. The deep brown shutters provide visual emphasis and balance the dark-stained wood front door.

In New Orleans, a popular candidate for renewing is the "shotgun double," a duplex so called because if a person fired a shot through the front door it would travel the length of the house. The version shown *at lower right* doesn't bring to mind the same kind of preconceived color notions as the Cape Cod Colonial shown above it. Here the owners wanted understated elegance, with a touch of Victorian charm. So they painted the body of their home a soothing, practical, and very attractive gray. Then they chose a dark slate gray for the shutters and clear white for the porch pillars, lintels, and other

trim. Finally, they outlined much of the detailing in deep purple. The result is a spruced-up old home that suits both the young owners' tastes and the home's own history.

The exuberantly colorful Victorian town house pictured *opposite* is a fine example of the Italianate style popular in the mid-nineteenth century. The color scheme—perhaps a bit unexpected to the late twentieth-century eye—is typical of the period, too. The olive siding is in keeping with the Victorian taste for deep-toned body colors. The blue, red, and black detailing above and below the bay windows shows Victorian variety at its best. Pristine white woodwork balances the strong colors used elsewhere and emphasizes the carvings and curlicues that give the structure so much of its character.

SPECIAL DETAILS
DESERVE
SPECIAL ATTENTION

Eighteenth- and nineteenth-century craftsmanship flowered in the lavish application of exterior details—made of wood, stone, and, later, metal—to buildings of all types. Whether you call these details frills, trim, embellishments, or gingerbread, they are key features of old-house charm.

The art of house ornamentation reached a peak during the late Victorian era, but even the more restrained architecture of earlier periods featured intricate detailing on columns, pediments, pilasters, and eaves.

Much of the wood trim used on early-vintage houses was hand-hewn. Today, for those who want reproductions of these features, machines turn out architectural ornaments in easily assembled form. What the new versions may lack in romance they often make up for in convenience and affordability.

Wrought iron, stonework, and terra-cotta also were lovingly crafted to add texture and design distinction to houses of various periods. Fewer examples have survived and reproductions are less widespread, and for that reason, details of these materials are perhaps to be cherished more than the more familiar wooden scrolls and gingerbread. They, too, can be repaired or replaced, although with somewhat more effort than it takes to find a milled wooden part.

Old trim that's been removed from the house it originally decorated is often available from architectural salvage dealers and sometimes even at antique shops. For more about finding replacement parts for a home's architectural details, see pages 80-81 and 136-137.

Upscale, downscale

The photos shown here illustrate how the widespread use of architectural ornamentation crossed social and economic lines.

The graceful paired brackets pictured *opposite* and the curvilinear window trim shown *at lower right* are both parts of the elaborate decorative scheme on an elegant 1860s Long Island mansion. The brackets emphasize the lines of the home's mansard roof. From ground level, their graceful scroll shape adds interest to a square-built house; on closer inspection, more subtle detailing—a pair of smaller scrolls at the base of each bracket and X-shaped carvings on the upper and lower faces of each bracket—becomes apparent. Similarly, the curved lintel of the two-over-two window set into the roof is only part of the window's charm. Subtle ribbonlike moldings extend down each side of the window trim to end in unusual and very appealing curlicues.

Exterior decoration was not just for the homes of the wealthy in the nineteenth century. The lacy triangle of Queen Anne gingerbread shown *at upper right* crowns an otherwise simple and relatively unadorned 1880s tract house.

Here, the details have been restored after decades of neglect. Contrasting paint colors make the most of the design and reflect the new owners' pride in their home. (Turn to page 70 to see the whole house; take special note of the simple but gracefully turned porch columns shown there.)

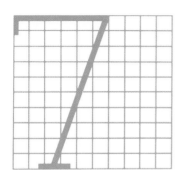

RENEWING INTERIORS

Your home's exterior is a public face that must relate to neighboring homes, comply with zoning ordinances, and possibly honor history as well. But inside a renewed home, you have considerably more leeway. Here you can choose to: (A) open up a floor plan, remove walls, and usher in a new era; (B) lovingly take the home back to its roots; or (C) steer a course somewhere in between. Follow us now on a tour through more than a dozen renovations and restorations to see differing approaches to walls, ceilings, stairs, windows and doors, fireplaces, and woodwork.

DOWN WITH WALLS FOR A BOLD NEW LOOK

Not all old homes boast grand ceiling heights, gracious rooms, and efficient floor plans. All too often an otherwise appealing house is burdened with a warrenlike layout of small, dark rooms connected by numerous hallways. Sometimes tearing out just a few walls can gain more usable space without actually adding square footage.

For example, the sleek look and open-plan design of the living room shown *opposite* belie the home's exterior—a 60-year-old brick cottage that's as old-fashioned as this room is contemporary.

A sturdy structure and the potential additional space offered by an unfinished attic inspired the owners to purchase the house and remodel it. "Before" and "after" floor plans *below* show what happened.

Removing two partition walls joined what had been a bedroom with the living room. Opening up the ceiling over both areas created the high, wide, and handsome new space shown *opposite*. Painting supporting beams white blended them with the walls and new cathedral ceiling. (For another view of this space, see page 107.)

At the rear of the house, closing in a screened porch and merging it with the kitchen and breakfast room created a spacious work area. New stairs lead to the finished attic, where a master suite and study overlook the living area.

If you're thinking about moving or removing walls, first determine what type of walls you're dealing with. *Bearing* walls run perpendicular to joists and rafters and are integral parts of a home's support structure. *Nonbearing* walls run parallel to joists and rafters, and support nothing but themselves. If you have any doubts, consult an architect or contractor.

(continued)

BEFORE

AFTER

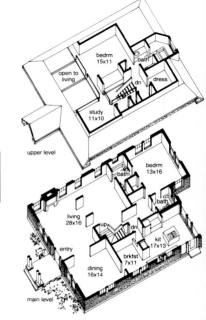

DOWN WITH WALLS FOR A BOLD NEW LOOK
(continued)

In the home shown on the preceding pages, the owners minimized costs by removing only nonbearing walls. Here the owner didn't let structural considerations stand in the way of his freewheeling plan. Instead, he gutted a deteriorated turn-of-the-century city house and started over again.

Removing the roof of an exterior front porch let light stream through tall windows set into recessed niches in the lofty two-story living area shown *at right.* Previously, a full-height wall had separated the living room and stairway. The owner opted to go through rather than around this obstacle. What remains of the original wall backs up to a new curving fireplace that keeps extra logs handy and gracefully steers traffic from the stairs into the living room.

New supporting beams and posts, downplayed as background, carry on the structural role of the removed wall. An oak-topped mantel winds into a former bedroom that's now an eating area. There the mantel becomes a serpentine half wall separating the dining room and stairs.

From the fireplace, an exposed flue runs up past a new loft bedroom/office, which was carved from a garret already graced with a high ceiling.

Structural matters are only one factor to consider when you think about removing walls, ceilings, and important architectural details. Restoration buffs argue that once these elements are gone, they can never be replaced. But if interior features were undistinguished to begin with—or are in very poor condition—you may have little choice other than a total renovation. For a look at a home that falls between these two extremes, turn the page.

SOMETHING OLD,
SOMETHING NEW

The owners of the homes featured on the preceding four pages wanted contemporary interiors with lots of light and open space. You can, however, brighten the interior of an older home and still preserve its original character. The house shown here is a case in point.

About a century ago a California farmer and his family might have been sitting around the fireplace in the living room shown *opposite*. Now the home is in an urban San Francisco neighborhood that's being renewed by a new generation of enterprising homesteaders.

The house had no hallways, which meant walking through rooms to get from one to another. The owners decided to live with the problems of the basic room layout (offset in part by a rear entrance to the kitchen), but do their best to improve traffic flow.

In the living room, this meant removing three doors that had shut it off from the rest of the house (see floor plans *at lower right* and reshaping the openings into tall graceful archways that echo the shape of the fireplace.

Cutting down the rear wall of the dining room to half-size and removing another door between the dining room and kitchen opened the view from the living room all the way through to the former back porch, which is now a breakfast room. To maintain an old-fashioned look, the owners paneled both the new dining room serving bar and the kitchen shown *at upper right* with salvaged sheathing boards.

Removing the kitchen ceiling and installing rooftop skylights brought the sun into this formerly dismal work area. A gridwork of dark-stained beams camouflages the modern skylights without blocking their light. Festooned with cookware and antiques, the beams form a giant pot rack that compensates for a shortage of closed storage.

BEFORE

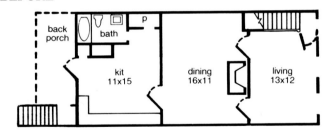

AFTER

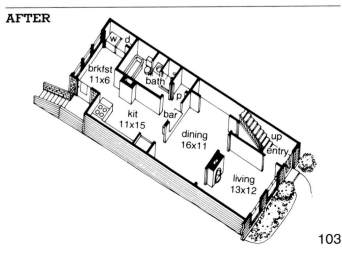

If the house you've slated for renewal has had many previous owners, its floor plan may reflect diverse and sometimes incompatible impulses. Houses that have grown with a series of additions often have awkward traffic plans. Creating a hallway by adding on or by reshuffling interior walls can provide easy access to rooms, help define activity zones, and increase both privacy and livability.

Before the present owners bought the 1850s District of Columbia town house shown here, it had become a rundown rooming house. Turning it from a derelict structure into a sophisticated and livable home meant combating general deterioration and—most important—remedying a severe traffic problem.

Originally two rooms deep and three stories high, the town house was five rooms deep by the 1970s, as illustrated in the "before" plan *below*. Getting from the front door to the kitchen meant walking through every room on the main floor. Upstairs, also because of a network of interconnected rooms, the house suffered similar traffic woes.

The architect's solution was to remove old porches and odd enclosures on the left side of the house and build a 29x7-foot gallery. Two stories high, the new gallery links the front of the house with the rear on the upper and lower floors. Abundant windows let this area double as a greenhouse.

Having this new access corridor enabled the homeowners to turn the former walk-through parlor into the peaceful library shown *at left*. The library also serves as a second, informal living room.

Believing they would discover a fireplace hidden inside the parlor/pantry wall, the owners decided to open it up. They found nothing, but decided to stick to their original vision by installing a heat-circulating unit where they had expected to find the fireplace. The new unit, sheathed in drywall, divides the library and a bar from the sitting room without obstructing the view between the areas.

BEFORE

AFTER

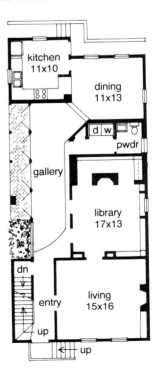

CEILINGS

Ceilings are as crucial as walls in defining interior spaces, both new and old. The builders of many old homes applied decorative treatments and architectural details overhead. Moldings, coves, raised plaster ornamentation, pressed metal, stencils, and wallpaper borders graced many a pre-World War II ceiling. Restoring these details is one exciting option. Another possibility, especially if you have a low ceiling that lacks embellishment, is to open up the room to the rafters. Either way, set your sights high for stunning results.

Some old houses are blessed with high ceilings that their original owners went to great lengths to adorn. For example, the ceiling pictured *at left* may look as if it's been papered, but actually it's decorated with a grid of flowers painstakingly hand-painted, one rosette at a time. Less ambitious home artists can achieve a similar effect with stencils or wall covering. Many museums and living-history villages offer stencil kits of authentic old patterns.

Decorative pressed metal, a delightfully ornate building

material, was popular around the turn of the century and is now enjoying a revival. Besides their nostalgic appeal, pressed metal ceilings are attractive, easy to install, and relatively inexpensive. First used in the mid-1800s to cover hopelessly damaged plaster ceilings, they can do the same today. Metal ceiling panels usually come in 2x8-foot sheets; you also can purchase lightweight sheet metal crown moldings. Though the metal is new, the dies used to stamp it are original to the period when the style was popular. You'll find a wide range of designs from detailed Victorian patterns to simple geometrics.

The photo *opposite, below* shows a new kitchen installation of pressed metal. In this case the metal was painted, but you also can coat it with clear polyurethane for a shiny bare metal look.

Instead of covering it up, you may prefer to repair an old plaster ceiling. If the key (the bond between the lath and plaster) is broken, remove the old plaster and replaster. Retaining the original plaster calls for more extensive and difficult repairs best done by a professional.

Rather than replaster, you could install a new drywall ceiling. For a really dramatic space reorganization, remove the ceiling entirely. The room shown *at right* (and on page 99) started out with low, unremarkable ceilings. The owners brightened the space by opening the ceiling to the roof line. To give this room a thoroughly contemporary look, the beams were painted unobtrusive white. In a more traditional setting, the beams could be stained or painted a contrasting color to become important design elements.

STAIRS

A venerable old hand-carved stairway can be the *pièce de résistance* of a restored house. But don't save a creaky, unsafe, or unsightly stairway simply out of nostalgia. If you're a proud owner of a worthy stairway, you probably want to repair, strip, and refinish it; in extreme cases, you could decide to totally disassemble and rebuild it. Or, if you lean toward a more modern interpretation of the interior, a new stairway can complement the contemporary mood of your renovation.

Stairways do far more than connect the floors of a house—they also reflect its history and character. From the simple turnings of a Georgian railing to ornately carved Victorian newel posts, stairway elements reflect the craftsmanship and aesthetics of each era in a dramatic way.

The elegant and stately carved stairway *at left* is the centerpiece of this vintage home. Layers of paint were stripped from the posts, rails, and balusters to reveal the warm natural tones of the beautiful cypress hidden beneath. This labor of love restored the classic stairway to its rightful prominence as the entry's focal point.

Old stairways often need structural repairs as well as surface improvements. The best way to fix sagging steps or problems in the stairway carriages or stringers is from underneath. If this is not possible, you'll have to remove the treads for access. Wood shims between the stringer and tread can remedy slight sagging or settling. Strengthen a weak stringer by gluing or bolting a new piece of wood to it. Repair squeaky treads with ring-shank nails; replace or restore worn treads by turning over the old tread to expose the underside.

If aesthetics dictate a new stairway with a modern look, consider opening up a center-hall home with a striking stairway, like the one shown *opposite*. Removing the original stairwell's walls opened the living room in the background to a music room in the foreground. To avoid obstructing the view, the owners chose a no-railing design with oak treads and trim.

Much of the charm of early-day homes is reflected in the fine woodwork and elegant proportions of their windows and doors. Multi-paned, and richly carved, arched, or embellished with leaded or stained glass, yesteryear's doors and windows were designed with more than just function in mind. The ravages of time, weather, and use often have left them in need of repair, but with patience, these vital elements can—and should—be renewed.

Before you tackle your home's windows and doors, do some research. Were they originally painted, or did the builder use attractive wood meant to be clear-finished?

In the living room pictured *opposite*, the floor-to-ceiling double-hung windows had originally been painted. They needed only minor scraping and two new coats of crisp white paint. Oxford gray walls bring them into sharp relief. Undraped for extra impact, the

windows frame a city view that becomes the focus of this inviting room. Look carefully and you'll see the original solid-pane shutters mounted inside the window casings. At night these close for greater privacy.

In the Victorian living room shown *below*, the windows and doors originally had been left natural, though decades of paint and grime had obliterated their glow. Gallons of paint stripper and lots of elbow grease brought the wood back to life. Restored cypress mold-

ings adorn the tops of the old door and living room window.

Whatever the visual end result you're seeking, windows and doors are mechanical elements and often must be restored to good working order. With double-hung windows, you may have to strip built-up layers of paint to unfreeze them and install new sash cords or chains for easy movement. Damaged panes must be replaced, and the frames recaulked. Plane sticky doors for smooth operation.

FIREPLACES

One of the most inviting features of an old house, a fireplace also could be a hazard and/or a big waster of energy. If your restored fireplace is going to play a solely decorative role, you need only close off its flue so furnace-warmed air doesn't escape through the fireplace and up the chimney. If, however, your aim is a working fireplace, you or a professional will have to ensure that all parts, including the chimney and chimney cap, damper, and firebox, are in safe operating condition. Be aware, too, that almost all old-fashioned fireplaces virtually "eat" energy, because the oxygen they need for combustion comes from the already-heated household air.

Many old fireplaces were sealed up years ago, and with good reason. Using a fireplace without a damper or a flue liner almost certainly will squander energy and could set fire to the house as well.

Restoring any old fireplace always requires thoroughly cleaning debris and creosote from the flue liner. How much more work is involved mainly depends on the condition of the flue liner. If it's not safe, or if your chimney was built without a liner, you may have to tear away and rebuild much of the chimney, a job demanding good masonry skills.

After you've ensured that all functional parts are in working order, you can turn an eye to appearances—restoring old brick that has been painted or plastered, for example. As shown *opposite*, the result can be a cozy focal point, such as the fireplace in this updated hacienda. The raised brick hearth, stuccoed chimney, and simple pine mantel make an almost sculptural grouping.

The more formal sitting room shown *at upper left* owes much of its grace to a carved marble mantel. This coal-burning fireplace is original to the home, an early-nineteenth-century Savannah town house. You may be able to find a similar treasure at auctions or through an antique or architectural salvage dealer.

Not all older houses come equipped with either chimneys or fireplaces. But you can add them. Owners of the refurbished cottage shown *at left, below* installed a new prefab, heat-circulating fireplace as part of their renovation. The exposed flue and drywall surround give it a look that's in keeping with the remodeling's contemporary flavor.

OLD WOODWORK

Restoring woodwork can be a soul-trying and finger-aching experience, but if you love fine old wood, the end results will seem well worth the effort. Restoration involves removing layers of finish or paint down to the bare wood and refinishing. To do this, you'll usually brush on a chemical stripper and remove the softened finish with appropriately shaped scrapers. Next, you need to go over the area with steel wool to remove all residue, rinse the surface, and let it dry. Then lightly sand the woodwork and apply a new finish of polyurethane, oil, or varnish.

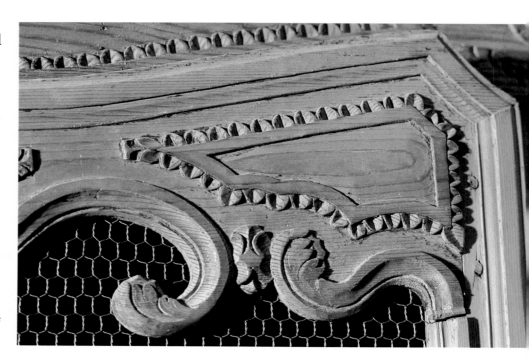

Hidden beneath all that paint, you may find a variety of woods ranging from pine and oak to rosewood, teak, mahogany, cedar, cherry, poplar, walnut, maple, birch, and cypress. The more expensive woods appear most frequently in grander old homes and in "public" rooms like the front parlor or entrance hall. Originally, the wood may have been stained, varnished, shellacked, oiled, waxed, painted, fumed, or even left unfinished. You may choose to restore to period accuracy, or simply select a finish that enhances the grain of the wood and the style of the woodwork.

If wood has been intricately hand carved, like the detailing on the china cupboard pictured *opposite, above,* you've got your work cut out for you. If you examine the photo closely, you can see slight remnants of the paint that once covered the now-natural pine. You'll need an assortment of small picks, knives, spatula-type tools, and patience to remove paint from the crevices.

Most interior trim was machine-planed at a mill rather than hand carved. Millwork includes door and window jambs, sills, sashes, mantels, mullions, muntins, stairway treads, risers, balusters, newels, and baseboard and cove moldings. Sometimes renewing millwork involves more than stripping and refinishing. If the wood is damaged beyond salvage, you'll need to reconstruct new millwork to match the original style. The plinth block, shown *opposite, below,* is a reconstruction modeled after nineteenth-century moldings intact elsewhere in the house. Compare it with an original, shown *at right*, which has been salvaged from another home, stripped of shellac and paint, and refinished.

CONTEMPORARY MILLWORK

Just because a house is old doesn't guarantee that its woodwork exemplifies fine old craftsmanship. In some houses the original woodwork was of poor quality; in others, it is so damaged it must be replaced. If your taste leans toward the contemporary, take a look at the outstanding updated treatments shown here.

Thanks to a revival of interest in woodworking, finding a skilled carpenter to execute quality millwork is no longer an impossibility. The selection of stock molding and millwork from manufacturers is also excellent. (More about this on pages 134-137.) What's more, you needn't stick with old-fashioned woodwork. Skylights, for example, are contemporary amenities that demand contemporary detailing. As the photographs *at right* illustrate, oak beams within a skylight can add character and make a perfect place to hang sun-loving plants. Though nonstructural, the beams make a solid decorative impact.

The single beam *at upper right* emphasizes the slope of a cathedral ceiling-window. Here a standard 2x6 joist was sheathed with oak lumber on the sides and bottom, then decorative oak trim was added.

A similar treatment brings architectural interest to the light shaft shown *at lower right.* Here fluorescent tubes recessed into two sides of the shaft brighten the room after sundown.

The arched window treatment shown *opposite* opened a formerly dark room to a sunburst of light. It's an exciting example of how daring to be different can pay handsome dividends.

Contemporizing the interior millwork of an old house requires the courage to experiment with designs and materials, and a commitment to quality in all finishing details. Your reward: a home revitalized with the stamp of your own personality.

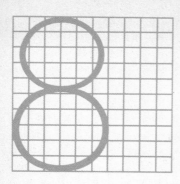

8

UPDATING MECHANICAL SYSTEMS

Renewing an older home's major household systems—heating and cooling, wiring, and plumbing—may seem like unglamorous work compared to the more visible satisfactions of restoring old millwork or refurbishing fine wood floors. Yet upgrading, repairing, or even replacing these largely hidden networks of pipes, ducts, and wires is absolutely essential if your house is to function efficiently and safely. This chapter will introduce you to the basics of each and show how to put them in good working order.

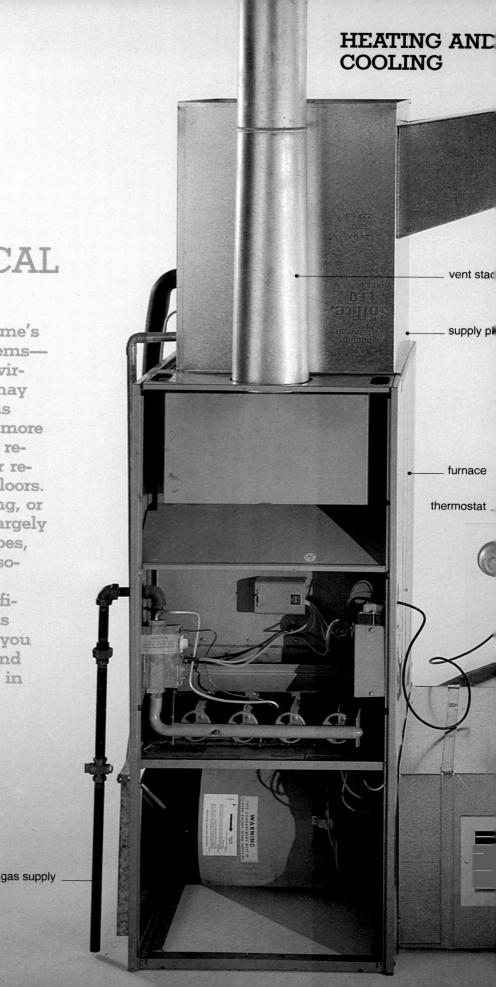

vent stac

supply p

furnace

thermostat

gas supply

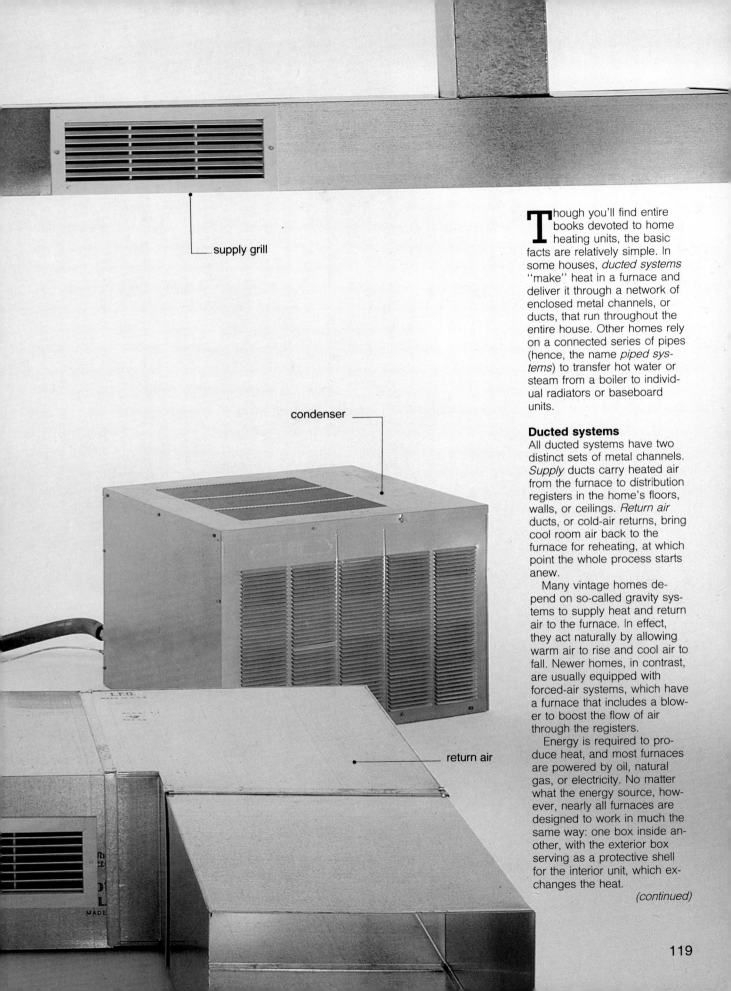

supply grill

condenser

return air

Though you'll find entire books devoted to home heating units, the basic facts are relatively simple. In some houses, *ducted systems* "make" heat in a furnace and deliver it through a network of enclosed metal channels, or ducts, that run throughout the entire house. Other homes rely on a connected series of pipes (hence, the name *piped systems*) to transfer hot water or steam from a boiler to individual radiators or baseboard units.

Ducted systems

All ducted systems have two distinct sets of metal channels. *Supply* ducts carry heated air from the furnace to distribution registers in the home's floors, walls, or ceilings. *Return air* ducts, or cold-air returns, bring cool room air back to the furnace for reheating, at which point the whole process starts anew.

Many vintage homes depend on so-called gravity systems to supply heat and return air to the furnace. In effect, they act naturally by allowing warm air to rise and cool air to fall. Newer homes, in contrast, are usually equipped with forced-air systems, which have a furnace that includes a blower to boost the flow of air through the registers.

Energy is required to produce heat, and most furnaces are powered by oil, natural gas, or electricity. No matter what the energy source, however, nearly all furnaces are designed to work in much the same way: one box inside another, with the exterior box serving as a protective shell for the interior unit, which exchanges the heat.

(continued)

119

HEATING AND COOLING
(continued)

Gas and oil furnaces operate with burners located inside the heat exchanger, which is always vented to the outside. Unvented electric units, on the other hand, don't have burners; instead, they heat with a set of electric-resistance elements similar to those in a toaster.

When a thermostat calls for heat, the burner comes on and starts to warm the heat exchanger. (In an electric furnace, the heating elements begin to phase in at this stage, one at a time.) Once the exchanger reaches a certain temperature, the blower kicks in, drawing air through the return ducts and sending it across the outside surface of the exchanger, where it is warmed. The heated air then rises or is blown through the supply ducts into the house.

Piped systems
Piped systems depend on water—hot liquid or steam—to distribute heat. Like their ducted counterparts, they can be either gravity or forced systems. In many hot-water systems, a pump does the same job a blower does in a forced-air unit.

Steam systems usually employ a "one-pipe" distribution method, which means that a single line both supplies steam heat to radiators or baseboard heaters and returns condensed water to the boiler for reheating. Some steam systems and practically all hot-water systems use a "two-pipe" arrangement whereby water enters and leaves radiation units via separate lines.

In each case, boilers creating the heat are similar in design and function. Like furnaces, they can be fired by gas or oil burners or powered by electric-resistance elements. In addition, every hot-water

system has an expansion tank partially filled with air. The air serves as a cushion that prevents heated water from boiling.

Evaluating and upgrading heating plants
You can pretty well guess the age of a furnace or boiler just by looking at it. If the basement of an old house is inhabited by a heavy iron or steel creature that resembles an immense, upside-down octopus, the unit probably dates back to the 1920s or earlier. Many heating plants from that era were originally fired with coal and converted to gas or oil later. Some old-time furnaces and boilers seem determined to run forever, but they all gobble prodigious amounts of fuel by today's standards. Replace an old monster with a modern-day, energy-efficient unit, and you can expect to recover your investment in the form of heating cost savings in three to five years.

Newer furnaces and boilers—usually jacketed in enameled sheet metal—are often one-third the size of their ancestors. Though more energy-thrifty, they typically last only 20-30 years, which means that a furnace or boiler installed in the 1950s or early 1960s may be nearing the end of its life. Again, replacing the unit may pay off in big energy savings.

Regardless of your heating plant's age, you should have it checked out by a heating specialist. Most, for a flat fee, will inspect a unit for safety and energy efficiency and estimate how much time it has left.

If the verdict is that you should replace a furnace or boiler, consider upgrading

your entire heating system, or possibly even switching to another medium. You might, for example, decide to convert a noisy, hard-to-regulate steam system to hot water or forced air. If your home has an electric-resistance furnace, a heat pump, which extracts heat from the air outside, might perform far more efficiently. Now's a good time, too, to investigate whether an active or passive solar installation could save big money in operating costs.

Before you can determine how much your renewed house might benefit from an entirely new heating system, you will have to analyze how well the current system distributes heat.

Evaluating and upgrading ductwork
The best way to evaluate a ducted heating system is to have a serviceman put the furnace in good working order, turn it on, and make a room-by-room survey of your home. Are some rooms or sections of rooms too cold, while others are too hot? If so, perhaps you can balance temperatures by adjusting air registers or by maneuvering dampers in main supply ducts leading from the furnace.

If that doesn't work, try to trace the paths hot air travels from the furnace to living areas. In some older homes, especially those built without central heating and converted later, supply ducts rise through or along inside walls; they should be at the home's perimeter. Old-time gravity systems, even those to which a blower was added later, may suffer from another problem. Their ducts are often too large to fully benefit from the advantage a blower offers.

If your basement has an open-joist ceiling, replacing or

extending main supply ducts—known as *plenums*—isn't difficult. If, however, you also need new *risers* to the rooms upstairs, your heating contractor will have to open up walls to install them, or you'll have to box in ducts after his workers leave.

Evaluating and upgrading piped systems
Analyze steam or hot-water heating in the same way you would a forced-air system—by turning on the boiler and checking each radiator in the house. If one doesn't heat up, even though its supply valve is open, you can be fairly sure that either air or water is trapped inside.

● *Steam radiators* expel air with each heating cycle. Rising steam pushes out air ahead of it through a *quick valve* located at the end of a radiator opposite its supply inlet. You may hear this valve hiss when steam is coming up, or feel air escaping with your hand. If no air comes out, the valve is defective and must be replaced.

Steam radiators also suffer when water is trapped inside. Incoming steam, hitting against condensed water, causes banging; in some cases, trapped water prevents steam from entering a radiator at all. To check for trapped water, lay a level atop the radiator. If only one pipe enters the radiator, the radiator should be pitched slightly toward that pipe; if it's not, shim up the far end so the unit slopes toward the supply pipe. If a steam radiator has two pipes, one at each end, tilt the radiator *away* from its supply valve.

• *Hot-water radiators* have a different type of air-release valve, one that's operated with a screwdriver or special key. Air needs to be bled from a hot-water radiator only once a year or so. You turn on the heat, open the valve until water begins to come out, and close the valve.

Regardless of whether your system is steam or hot water, examine its piping carefully. Are valves and fittings corroded? Do the pipes themselves, especially horizontal runs, look as if they're rusting from the inside out? The steel pipes in heating systems have a life-span of about 50 years. If yours are that old or older, you might be wise to replace everything, excepting perhaps vertical runs. (Vertical runs aren't prone to severe rusting because water doesn't stand in them.)

If you discover that you must replace all or most of a piped system, consider upgrading it or changing it entirely to something different. Steam heat, for example, can be converted to hot water, which allows for more control over temperature. You may be surprised to discover that the big expense in converting from steam to hot-water heating lies not with the boiler (the same units, with slightly different accessories, serve as heating plants for both), but with the distribution network. Piping sizes and configurations differ, as do radiation units.

Another reason for completely replacing a piped system might be that you want to add central air conditioning. Then you might decide to convert to forced-air heating. More about this in the box at right.

COOLING AN OLD HOUSE

Depending on how cool you want to be and how much you're willing to pay for it, cooling an older home can be anything from a breeze to a very expensive proposition. Here are your three main options.

• *Passive cooling* relies on nonmechanical features, such as shading and natural air currents. Houses that are 50 years old or older often boast big windows, plenty of cross-ventilation, high ceilings, well-developed trees, and other features that minimize heat buildup. Air that's moving can lower skin temperatures by as much as 10 degrees. Depending on your climate and tolerance for heat, this may be enough to make bearable all but the hottest days of summer, especially if you supplement natural airflow with low energy users such as ceiling and attic fans. Be warned, though, that passive cooling does nothing about humidity, and, as the old saying goes, often "it ain't the heat, it's the humidity" that makes you uncomfortable. Passive cooling for an older home requires little or no investment and costs next to nothing to operate.

• *Room air conditioners* let you cool selected areas of a home. Combined with passive techniques, such as fans strategically located to move conditioned, dehumidified air through adjacent areas, just a few room air conditioners could effectively cool and dehumidify an entire home. What's

more, you can shut off a room air conditioner when you're not using a space, which can save considerably on operating costs. Another cost advantage to cooling a home room-by-room is that you can buy room air conditioners one at a time, though you may have to invest additional money in bringing power to bigger units, especially in older homes where the electrical system is already marginal. (More about this on pages 122-125.)

• *Central air conditioning* is normally tied into a forced-air heating system, circulating cool, dehumidified air through the system's supply ducts. The cooling cycle actually starts elsewhere, however, at a *condenser* located outside the house. Here a hot refrigerant gas is cooled, transformed into a liquid, and sent through copper tubing to an *evaporator coil* attached to the furnace. The blower then moves air through the coil—cooling and drying it in the process—and boosts the now-conditioned air into the supply system. The refrigerant, a hot gas once more, returns to the condenser for another cycle.

Central air conditioning is the most expensive solution. If your home is now heated with steam or hot water, you'll have to run ductwork. Even if your home already has forced-air heating, its ducts may not be quite large enough to efficiently circulate cooled air, which is heavier than warm air.

Besides the costs of changing the ductwork, including the associated carpentry costs, installing central air conditioning requires that you purchase and maintain a condenser and evaporator coil, along with the tubing that runs between them. Operating costs can run higher, too, than they might be for room air conditioners, and certainly higher than the negligible cost of passive cooling.

Hybrid cooling systems
If yours is a one- or two-story home with a serviceable piped heating system, you might be able to reduce the cost of a central air conditioning installation by locating ducts and an evaporator in the attic. In this case, the ducts would serve for cooling only and, in a two-story house, perhaps only rooms on the upper level would benefit. Main-level areas might be cooled with room air conditioners or passive techniques, assisted by any cool air that might spill down an open stairway.

WIRING

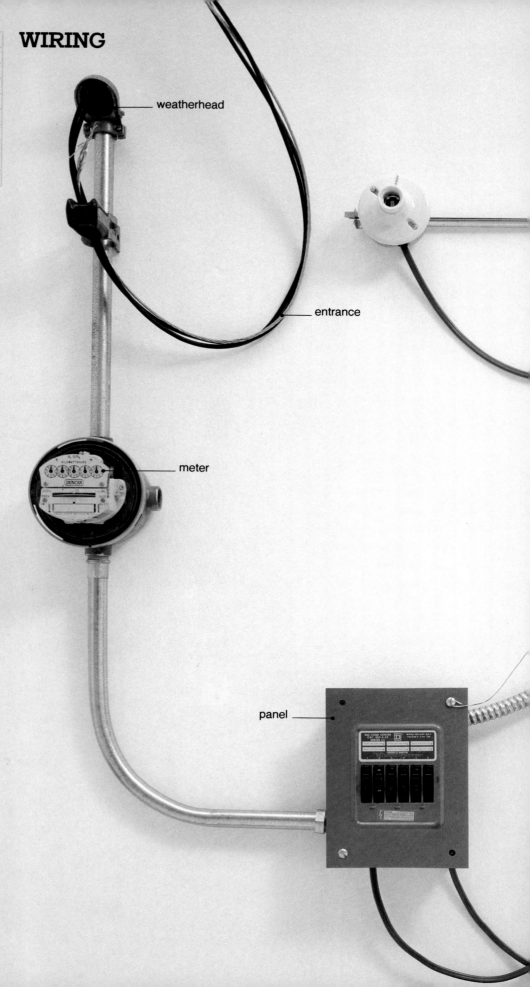

weatherhead

entrance

meter

panel

Electricity. To many, it's a sizzling, snapping, mysterious beast—tame enough in its wires behind the walls of a house but always ready to strike out and zap the unwary.

Like a lot of other things, electricity can be dangerous if you don't understand and respect its power. On the other hand, learning how it works doesn't require an engineering degree. In fact, the principles are fairly easy to grasp.

Electricity is made up of electrons, invisible particles of matter coursing at the speed of light through a network of wires in a house. These electrons always flow in circles called circuits.

Their circular path begins at a municipal power plant, where a generator sends out charged electrons. These go by way of overhead or underground wires to a home's service entrance.

The power flows through a *meter,* which monitors household consumption, and then proceeds to a *service panel,* where it's broken down into a series of circuits delivering current throughout the house. Here, fuses or circuit breakers control individual circuits, shutting them down if they receive more power than they're designed to handle.

Every possible exit from a circuit is called an *outlet,* which generally consists of a *receptacle, switch,* or *light.* When a toaster, for example, is plugged in and turned on, the electrons deliver their charges, powering the appliance into action, and then return to the service panel. Here they move to the original generator, or to the earth via a *ground,* an extremely important safety feature. *(continued)*

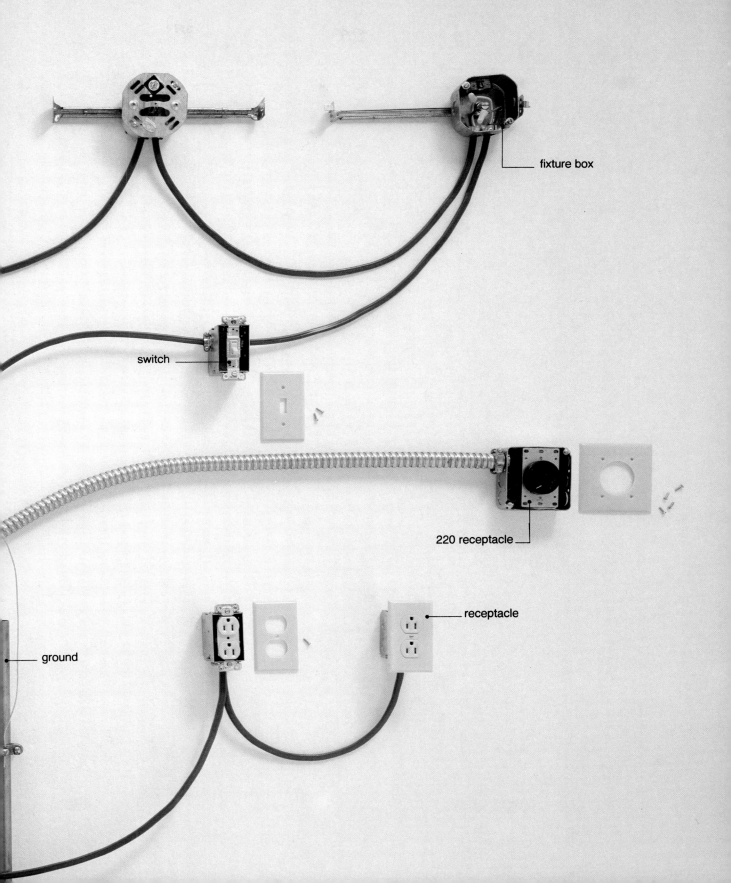

fixture box

switch

220 receptacle

ground

receptacle

WIRING
(continued)

Unless your home has recently been rewired, the components of its electrical system may only faintly resemble the up-to-date versions shown on the preceding pages. It's likely that your receptacles have only two slots, with no provision for grounding heavy-duty appliances. Switches may consist of a pair of push buttons, or amount to nothing more than pull chains dangling from light fixtures. And the service panel probably features fuses, not circuit breakers.

All of these elements are obvious and fairly easy to upgrade. But before you or an electrician can determine how extensive a rewiring job your home needs, you must assess the type and condition of the wires themselves.

What's inside the walls?
Most of a home's wiring is concealed in its walls, above ceilings, or under floors. You may notice exposed sections here and there—in the basement or attic, for example—but these could have been added during a modernization and may not be indicative of wiring you *can't* easily see. Though you'll have to do some patching afterward, the best way to get a good look at what's in your home's walls, ceilings, or floors is to open them up at several points and, with the aid of a flashlight, peer inside. The following describes what you might discover.
• *Knob-and-tube* wiring dates back to before the turn of the century and was extensively used in homes built before the 1930s. For each circuit a pair of cloth-and-rubber-covered wires follows separate but parallel courses. You may find one running along a stud or

joist and the other along another framing member on the opposite side of the wall or ceiling cavity. Porcelain *knobs* hold the wires away from wood surfaces; porcelain *tubes* protect wires where they pass through framing members. Wires converge only where they enter or leave an outlet box; at these points, they're sheathed with fabric tubing called *looms.*

Knob-and-tube wiring still serves millions of American homes, but in almost every one of them it presents a potential fire and safety hazard. Changes in temperature and humidity may have all but destroyed insulation that's more than 50 years old, and the wires themselves may be undersized for today's electrical needs. If your home has knob-and-tube wiring, plan to totally replace it.
• *Wood wireways* resemble ordinary wood moldings. Shut off the power, pry one away from a wall or ceiling, and you'll discover a pair of wires running along grooves in the back of the molding. Wood wireways also date back to early electrical history (often they were installed in homes that hadn't originally been wired for electricity). Like knob-and-tube wiring, wood wireways are obsolete and dangerous.
• *Fabric-covered cable* consists of a pair of rubber-covered wires sheathed with loosely woven fabric. Electrical codes typically don't permit the use of fabric-covered cable in new or rewiring jobs, but neither do they mandate that you replace it—provided the fabric hasn't grown tattered

and frayed or the wires' rubber coverings become brittle. Whether or not you should completely rewire a home served by fabric-covered cable is a judgment call, one you should consult with an electrician about before deciding.
• *Armored cable*—often called *BX*—became popular in the 1930s, and virtually all electrical codes still approve it for use inside walls and ceilings. With armored cable, rubber-coated wires run through a helix of twisted gray metal sheathing that protects the wires from physical damage. If you find armored cable, and your house is more than 50 years old, check at several other points in the electrical system; armored cable may have been used only for circuits that were added later, with fabric-covered cable or knob-and-tube wiring serving the others.

If all of your home's existing wiring consists of armored cable, count yourself fortunate. You may need to upgrade receptacles, switches, and the service panel—and run wiring for any new circuits your plans call for—but you won't have to rip into walls and replace all the wires inside.
• *Plastic-sheathed cable* dates back only 20 years or so. Insulated wires are encased in tough but pliable plastic. Plastic-sheathed cable, sometimes called "Romex", is a highly durable, up-to-date material, but not all electrical codes approve its use. If those in your area prohibit plastic-sheathed cable, any that might have been installed in your house will have to come out and be replaced with armored cable.

Evaluating exposed wiring
In contrast with the wires that run inside walls, ceilings, and floors, wiring in exposed

locations—such as across basement ceiling joists or from a switch to a light on a garage rafter—is easy to see and equally easy to assess. The only material that can be safely and legally used in exposed situations is *conduit,* a rigid metal tubing that can be bent to wrap around corners and curves. After the tubing is installed, rubber-covered wires are pulled through it.

If you find plastic-sheathed cable, armored cable, fabric-covered cable, wood wireways, or knob-and-tube wiring any place *outside* of walls, ceilings, and floors, it must be either rerouted or replaced with conduit.

Upgrading wiring
Even if your survey determines that all of the existing wiring in your home is safe and up-to-date, modern-day codes and convenience will probably demand that you add on to the electrical system. Older homes were typically under-wired by today's standards, with only one or two outlets per room, and not nearly enough circuits for contemporary needs. Snaking new wires for these outlets and circuits—and/or replacing obsolete wiring—can challenge the skill and patience of even a veteran electrician.

If you need to remove, move, or open up walls and ceilings anyway, that's clearly the time to install new wiring. If not, you'll still have to break into surfaces at strategic locations, then "fish" wires from one point to another. The trick is to develop a mental X-ray of the framing and other elements underneath your home's surfaces, then plan accordingly.

Fishing wires calls for an understanding of house carpentry, mastery of a few simple electrical procedures, resourcefulness—and luck. An electrician can bring additional power into a house and install a new service panel in a matter of hours. Maneuvering new wires through a home's hidden and sometimes mysterious labyrinths, on the other hand, can take days or even weeks, especially if you demand that surfaces and moldings suffer a minimum of damage.

For this reason, you can save considerably on the cost of electrical work by arranging with an electrician to provide you with a new service panel and doing the fishing yourself. After you've completed this time-consuming part of the job, the electrician can return, check out your work, and make final hookups.

Upgrading electrical service

As noted above, many old houses are under-wired, but they aren't necessarily under-*powered*. At the time it was constructed, a home may have been served by two wires from a utility company's pole and equipped with a meager 40- or 60-amp-capacity fuse box.

But electrical systems are easily patched onto. For instance, a family that lived in your house 30 years ago might have purchased an electric dryer and hired an electrician to bring in the 220-volt current it required. He probably ran new wires from the pole, three of them this time, and installed a new subpanel near the fuse box. Later, as households' appetites for electricity increased, additional subpanels might have been added for air conditioners or workshop equipment.

If electricity seems to come into your house through a miscellany of fuses and circuit breakers in assorted boxes, you may already have the 150 to 200 amps of power a modern home should have. Only an electrician can tell for sure. But even if you have adequate power, plan on consolidating all those panels and subpanels into one convenient bank of circuit breakers.

Upgrading receptacles, switches, and fixtures

Fishing wires is a job you might choose to take on yourself or hire an electrician to do. Upgrading service and installing a new service panel, however, should be handled only by a licensed electrician. The third and final phase of any rewiring project—installing new switches, receptacles, and light fixtures—is well within the capabilities of even a moderately skilled do-it-yourselfer.

Working always with the power off, you simply attach wires to each device, carefully tuck the wires and device into a wall or ceiling box, and tighten a couple of screws. Basic wiring books and instructions that come with the devices explain these procedures. After each device is installed, you then turn the circuit back on, assure that the new element works, and test to make sure that it's properly grounded, as explained in the box at right.

As the discussion on page 122 explains,

IS YOUR WIRING GROUNDED?

As the discussion on page 122 explains, electricity needs only two wires to energize a circuit. A *hot* wire, usually with either black or red insulation, brings current to an outlet; a *neutral* wire, which always wears white insulation, carries electricity from the outlet to the service entrance, and ultimately into the ground.

Virtually all modern-day codes require that you also provide a third pathway for electricity. Known as a *ground,* this one is designed to carry away errant electricity that might be leaking from a faulty motor or other device. With some wiring, the ground is a third wire that always has green insulation; with others, such as armored cable or conduit, the wiring's metal covering provides an unbroken route into the ground.

The reason for grounding is to protect you from serious electrical shock. Touch a malfunctioning appliance that's not grounded and that errant electricity could pass through your body on its way to the ground. Unfortunately, the electrical systems in many older homes are improperly grounded, and some provide no third route for electricity to travel.

You can test for grounding yourself. All you need is an inexpensive *neon test light,* a small neon bulb attached to two wire probes. With the cover plate off an outlet and the current on, touch one probe to a part of the electrical device you know is hot—this might be

either of the slots in a receptacle, or the black wire connected to a switch or fixture. Now touch the other probe to the electrical box or a strap or other metal element attached to the box. If the tester lights up, the box is grounded; if not, the outlet—and probably most others in your home—poses a shock hazard.

Ground fault circuit interrupters

Even properly grounded outlets could leak a tiny amount of electricity, though scarcely enough to give you a tickle under most circumstances. But let's say *you* happen to be exceptionally well grounded, as you might be when turning on a bathroom radio and a water faucet at the same time. Then that tiny bit of errant current could pass through your body on its way to the earth, and the shock could be fatal.

This is why recently revised electrical codes specify that circuits serving "wet" locations such as bathrooms, garages, and outdoor outlets must be equipped with *ground fault circuit interrupters (GFCIs).* A GFCI—some types replace ordinary outlets, others are installed near the service panel—automatically trips the circuit if there's any current leakage at all.

UPDATING
MECHANICAL
SYSTEMS

vent

heater

gas

servic

m

In contrast to the mechanical complexities of modern heating and cooling units, nearly all residential plumbing systems, old or new, are amazingly simple arrangements made up of two independent parts: *supply lines* and *drain-waste-vent lines*.

How each works is entirely uncomplicated. Water comes into a house through a large pipe, called the *service main,* that's connected to a municipal water line or to a private well. If it's city water, it flows through a *meter* designed to record the amount used. It then travels to a water heater or, in the case of a private well, to a pressure tank before moving on to the heater.

From there, a pair of small pipes, each carrying water under constant pressure, branches out to serve all the fixtures and water-using appliances in the house. These are the *supply* lines. One provides hot water; the other, cold.

Most supply pipes are outfitted with separate stop valves at the meter, water heater, and individual fixtures and appliances (though not every system has a valve for each sink or toilet). These can be turned off to shut down all or part of the water flow when repairs are necessary.

The drain-waste-vent lines, which are much larger than supply pipes, rely on gravity to move liquid and solid wastes out of the house (the drain-waste portion) and serve as an outlet for potentially noxious sewer gases (the vent part).

Except for toilets, every fixture has a trap at the head of the drainpipe. Here, water forms an impervious seal that stops sewer gases from escaping into the house.

(continued)

126

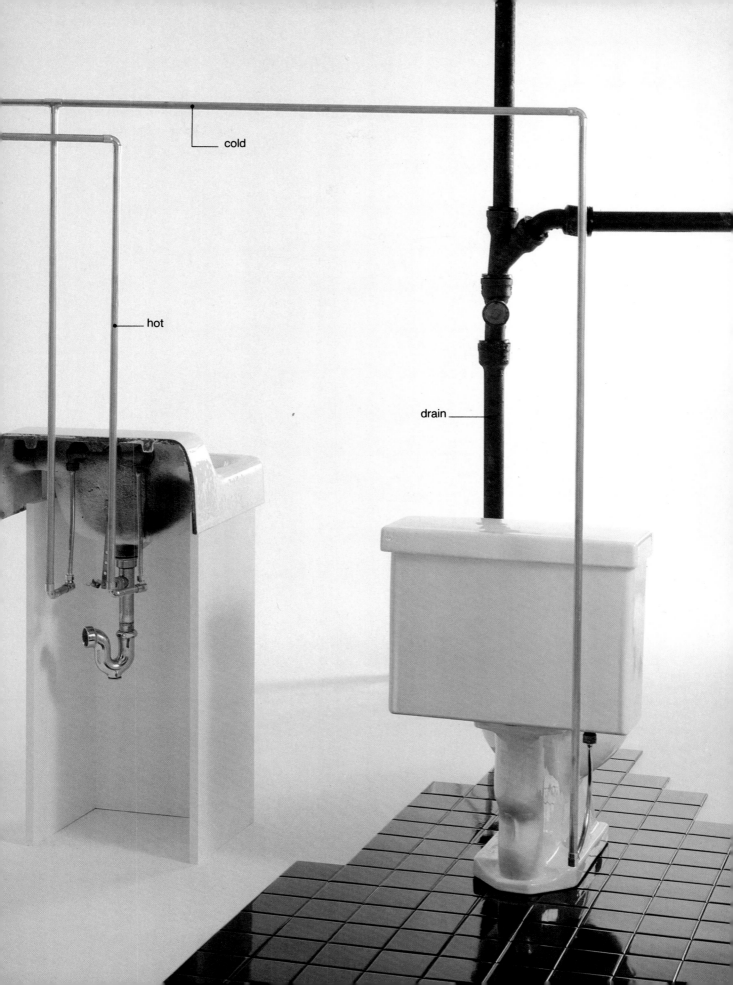

cold

hot

drain

PLUMBING
(continued)

Unlike most vintage electrical systems, elderly plumbing may be perfectly adequate for years to come. On the other hand, it's a good bet that at least part of the system—often many parts—will have to be upgraded or replaced, especially if you plan to change the location of bathrooms or a kitchen, or add new water-using appliances.

Evaluating water supply lines

First let's look at the plumbing lines that bring hot and cold water to fixtures. In old houses, these are made of galvanized steel, lead, copper, or—in a few cases—brass.

• *Galvanized steel* piping serves many older homes. It's strong and inexpensive, but tends to rust from the inside out. Corrosion builds up on the interiors of galvanized pipes, reducing the flow of water. The water takes on a rusty, brownish hue. Eventually, galvanized pipes spring leaks, especially at fittings and along horizontal runs. Even if galvanized steel supply lines seem to be holding up well, problems will surface sooner or later, probably sooner. Replacing them in the early stages of a renewing project, when you're likely to have the walls open anyway, is usually a savvy move.

• *Lead* pipes date back to the early days of indoor plumbing, and are surprisingly durable. If your home's water supply lines seem to be almost seamless, even at joints, they're probably made of lead. Lead is insoluble in water, which means it doesn't rust—and doesn't present toxic hazards, either. Because lead is soft, it can be either easy or difficult to repair. In some cases, you can stop a

pinhole leak by merely whapping the pipe with a hammer; squished lead plugs the leak. On the other hand, lead's softness makes it vulnerable to blows, and the torque from a wrench can wreck a pipe. If you have defective lead supply lines, hire a plumber, who will probably replace bad pipes, or the entire supply system, with another material.

• *Copper* pipes are a genuine treasure. Though infrequently found in homes more than 40 or 50 years old, they last much, much longer than galvanized steel, aren't as vulnerable to damage as lead, and, unless excessively hard water has clogged them badly, should continue to stand up almost indefinitely. If your home has galvanized or lead supply lines that must be replaced, consider having the job done with copper.

• *Brass* piping can be found inside the walls of a few older houses. Like lead, brass is soft and therefore can be physically damaged; like lead and copper, it's highly resistant to corrosion. Brass is expensive. If brass supply lines need to be extended or replaced, your plumber will probably recommend a different material.

Upgrading supply lines

What you choose to do about the supply lines in an old house depends partly on what condition they're in and partly on the extent of the modifications you plan to make to the home's plumbing system. If the old lines are in poor or dubious shape, or you'll be making a lot of changes, you may as well replace the entire system, back to the service entrance

(or even to the street), with new piping. If, on the other hand, supply lines are copper or brass, aren't leaking or otherwise defective, and go at least near to where you want them, your home's plumbing may need only minor surgery.

For new supply line work, your material choices boil down to just two: copper and plastic. Copper, as noted above, is very durable. It's also costly, however, and tricky to work with until you master the knack of sweat-soldering fittings together.

You won't find plastic pipes in an old house—unless it's been renewed recently. Only within the last couple of decades has plastic been a serviceable material for residential plumbing systems. First it was employed only for drainpipes; more recently it's serving for supply lines, as well. Plastic is almost as durable as copper, won't dent your pocketbook as badly, and, perhaps most important, is the only piping material average do-it-yourselfers can install on their own with a minimum of fuss and bother. Nevertheless, many local codes still strictly prohibit or limit its use, especially in supply line situations.

You'll find three basic kinds of plastic pipe:

• *ABS* (acrylonitrile butadiene styrene) can be used only for drain-waste-vent lines. More about this one below.

• *PVC* (polyvinyl chloride) can be used for DWV (drain-waste-vent) and cold water lines, but, because it's susceptible to expansion and contraction, PVC can't carry hot water.

• *CPVC* (chlorinated polyvinyl chloride) is the only plastic that can be used for hot water lines. It can carry cold water as well, but is more costly than PVC.

If codes in your locality permit the use of plastic for supply lines, by all means go ahead and use it. If not, specify that all new work be done in copper, which is approved by virtually all plumbing codes. With either material, it's important that you or your plumber use *transition fittings* at all points where new lines join old lines. With dissimilar metals, such as copper and steel, electrolytic action can cause corrosion at joints. Plastic is chemically inert and poses no such problem, but because it doesn't conduct electricity, and because metal water supply systems are often used as electrical grounds, any new plastic sections should be bridged with ground wires.

Controlling supply lines

Think of supply lines as small but powerful rivers of water coursing throughout your house. Like rivers over their banks, out-of-control supply lines can do a lot of damage when one breaks or springs a leak. Shut-off valves are designed to stop the flow, if necessary. For the best, most precise overall protection, most plumbers now recommend placing shut-off valves on every vertical riser, on pipe sections breaking off to serve the kitchen or bathroom, and on the line supplying water to each individual fixture—in addition, of course, to a main shut-off valve at the service entrance. The extra controls allow you to lock water away from relatively small parts of the system to make repairs without interfering with the flow to other parts of the house.

New supply lines should also come equipped with capped chambers near each fixture. These keep air in the system, thus preventing the irritating and potentially damaging condition called "water hammer."

Evaluating drain-waste-vent lines

Generally, you'll find cast-iron pipes forming this part of the plumbing system. Cast iron is an enormously rugged material, and if it's in good condition, there's no reason to make changes.

However, it's not uncommon to find that house settlement or past remodeling projects, done improperly, have weakened the system overall. If the main house drain is seriously clogged, you'll have to replace it, at which point the best advice is to install all new drain, waste, and vent pipes throughout the house. The same holds true if you're changing the arrangement of fixtures or adding a lot of new ones.

Fitting in new drainpipes is usually more difficult than installing new supply lines, both because drainpipes are larger and because, to let gravity work most effectively, they must drop about ¼ inch for every foot of pipe. (Main drains are an exception to this rule—they go straight up and down.) In addition, the flow of water slows down if the pipes turn too sharply as they descend from the fixtures, thereby making the whole system less efficient.

In all systems, both old and new, there should be clean-out plugs both at the base of the main drainpipe and in other easy-to-reach positions. Further, many vintage plumbing layouts lack a final trap at the point where wastes exit the house. Because protection here helps stop sewer gases from seeping up into the waste

pipes, it's a good move to make a house trap like this part of the drain-waste-vent system, even if you retain the original arrangement of pipes.

Upgrading DWV lines

On the face of it, selecting a material for a drain-waste-vent system shouldn't be difficult at all. Plastic pipe, either ABS or PVC, is simply the best, least expensive, and easiest-to-work-with material you can buy. Unfortunately, local plumbing codes may ban its use in residential systems.

If that's true where you live, the second-best material is the old standby, cast iron. Although it's practically invulnerable, cast iron is more expensive than plastic, is harder to install, and requires the strength of a champion weight lifter to move around. Nevertheless, you'll have to use it if codes don't permit plastic.

Fortunately, one recent development has made cast iron easier to work with. Formerly cast-iron pipes were connected with hub-type joints that had to be sealed with molten lead—definitely a job for a skilled plumber. With newer "no-hub" fittings, you simply butt pipe ends together, slip a neoprene sleeve over the joint, and compress the sleeve with an automotive-type hose clamp.

Copper, though it makes very serviceable supply lines, is far too costly for most drain-waste-vent systems. In any case, copper is exceptionally susceptible to corrosion caused by sewer gases.

Evaluating and upgrading gas lines

Though potentially the most dangerous parts of your home's plumbing system, gas lines are the easiest to evalu-

ate and improve. In all but some Victorian-era homes, where the lines may be made of brass, gas typically flows through ungalvanized steel pipes—called "black steel" or "black iron"—that last a century or more without problems. If you can see that all or a part of your gas lines are made of another material, especially galvanized pipe, you should definitely check with a plumber and ask that they be replaced. Otherwise, simply request a pressure test. The plumber shuts off all gas-using appliances—each should be equipped with a shut-off valve—forces air into the system with a compressor or bicycle-type pump, and attaches an air-pressure gauge. If the pressure drops within 15 minutes or so, there's a leak somewhere and each pipe and fitting will have to be checked until the leak is found.

Evaluating and upgrading fixtures

The only parts of a home's plumbing system that you see on a daily basis are its fixtures. Here, you can let your own preferences be your guide. Many a renewed home has brand-new pipes behind the walls, though you'd never know it by looking at the claw-foot tubs, chain-pull toilets, and old-fashioned pedestal-style sinks they're connected to. One exception is the old-time "wash-down" toilet—a type in which water and waste exit from the *front* of the bowl, usually with a loud "glug." These are unsanitary and prohibited by most modern-day codes. Also, though you may choose to recycle fixtures, plan on upgrading the faucets and other fittings that serve as their working parts. (More about this on pages 130 and 131.)

(More about this on pages 130 and 131.)

IS YOUR PLUMBING PROPERLY VENTED?

As mentioned on page 126, the *vent* portion of a home's drain-waste-vent system lets sewer gases escape from your home. In addition, because a main vent stack is open to the atmosphere at the roofline, it equalizes air pressures within the system. If pressures were not the same, water rushing from one fixture could suck the water from another fixture's trap. Without water in the trap, gases could back up through that fixture.

All home plumbing systems are vented to the roof, but in many older houses, individual fixtures are not properly tied into the main stack. If that's the case at your house, you may hear the kitchen sink drain, for example, gulp when a toilet is flushed upstairs.

To check a poorly vented fixture, shine a flashlight down the drain as the gulping occurs. Does the water level in the trap drastically recede, or disappear entirely? If so, venting should be modified to conform with codes.

Codes stipulate that new plumbing meet strict venting specifications but "grandfather" existing installations, as long as they're in good working order.

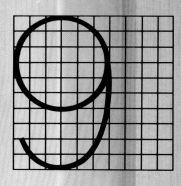

KEEPING UP APPEARANCES

Once you've dealt with systems that are largely unseen, you can turn your attention to things that show. For a period look, you need to strike a balance between authenticity, availability, price, and convenience. Here's an overview of what to consider and where to find it.

Finishing off an updated house with attractive and functional hardware presents few problems beyond choosing what you like. Finding appropriate fittings for a period restoration, however, requires that you find happy mediums between form and function.

For example, how much authenticity do you want in high-use rooms such as kitchens and baths? Can an eighteenth-century latch on the front door keep out twentieth-century burglars? What's the right way to equip and decorate a bath in a home that was built before indoor plumbing was standard?

Function first
When it comes to choosing plumbing items—faucets, drains, and other fittings—keep in mind that this hardware must be able to withstand *hard wear*. An antique faucet that

drips and leaks at the base probably will provide more authenticity than you bargained for. If you can be satisfied with something that just looks old, several manufacturers will come to your aid with catalogs full of well-researched, carefully crafted reproductions.

Unless you're willing to undertake a series of frequently frustrating expeditions to antique and architectural salvage dealers to find just the right hardware, you'll be better off sticking to reproductions of items whose smooth function is crucial. Keep in mind, too, that the ''right'' hardware has to fit with other components as much as it has to fit the period. A beautiful set of salvaged porcelain faucet handles, for example, probably will not fit on modern-day stems.

If your home still has its original faucets and fittings intact, it's possible, though not necessarily easy, to restore them to good working order. Besides thorough cleaning, the faucet may have to be replated, and its washers replaced. In some cases, the unit may have to be entirely rebuilt. A few plumbing companies stock old faucet parts and also will make parts to your specifications. But unless you live in or near a large metropolitan area, it's often difficult to find someone willing and able to do this kind of work.

If you choose reproduction hardware, the selection is excellent, but costly. With the popularity of Victorian renovation and restoration sweeping the country, hardware from this period is especially easy to come by. For baths and kitchens, you'll find a selection

of brass- and chrome-finish fittings and accessories for pedestal sinks, marble top lavatories, claw-footed tubs, and old-fashioned toilets. You can pair reproduction hardware, such as the faucet sets shown *at left*, with authentic cast-iron and porcelain fixtures whose surfaces have been cleaned and restored.

If your home predates indoor plumbing, you can't authentically restore a bathroom or kitchen unless you're willing to live with an outhouse and an outdoor water pump. In this case, you can opt for a totally modern bath and kitchen, or select simple, modern fixtures and hardware, and let period floor, wall, and window treatments integrate the room with the rest of the house.

Other hardware

If you'd like some genuine old items, look for door knockers, drawer pulls, interior latches, and other primarily decorative hardware.

Reproductions ranging from classic Colonial to high-style Victorian will help you fill in the gaps. For Early American settings, you'll find an abundance of wrought-iron hinges, shutter dogs, hooks, fireplace accessories, brackets and holders. For homes of a later vintage, reproduction door locks, knockers, knobs, escutcheons, and mail slots are available in both ornate and simple brass styles, such as those shown *opposite*.

Whatever hardware you select, getting a proper fit is crucial. The box at right explains how to measure for faucets and locks to ensure trouble-free installation.

GETTING A GOOD FIT

Hardware has changed with the times, and many fixtures already have holes for the faucets and drain. This means that any replacement components have to fit exactly.

Faucets are sized according to the distance from the center of the hot water inlet pipe to the center of the cold water inlet pipe. To find the distance between pipe centers that the holes in your fixture will accommodate, measure from the outside edge of one hole to the inside edge of the other. Plumbing catalogs also provide the distance from the center of the faucet to the spout, which tells you how far the spout projects into the basin. Measure the thickness of a sink top, too, and make sure the faucet you choose is compatible.

Locks

Replacing locks and latches poses special problems, too. If the new unit must be mortised into the door, it probably won't fit the original mortise; then you'll need to patch the old mortise with new wood and cut a new mortise. With luck, you can find an escutcheon that will cover the patch. In measuring for a new lock set, be sure to consider the door's thickness.

LIGHTING

Choosing the right lighting for an older home involves not only the appearance of the lamps and fixtures themselves, but also the kind of light they cast. Before the twentieth century, homes were lit by firelight, candles, oil, kerosene, or gas. Flickering candlelight creates an entirely different impression than does the bright steady illumination of a modern electric lamp. Gas light, though softer toned than most electric lights, is considerably brighter than the glow of an oil lamp.

If you are updating your home's interior, you can choose from a wide selection of modern electric incandescent or fluorescent lighting. But if your aim is a period atmosphere, typical modern lighting can be glaringly out of place. Knowing the kinds of lighting and fuel that were used when your home was built can help you set an appropriate mood. Most obviously, it will guide you in choosing antique lamps and fixtures, as well as authentic or authentic-looking reproductions appropriate to the era in which your home was built. You'll also get a sense of what level of illumination was common in earlier times. Modern homes are typically far brighter than their predecessors, and period decorating materials and colors often look their best under softer light. This doesn't mean that you have to give up electric lighting in a period setting, but it does mean that you have to use it thoughtfully.

Unless you discover old photographs, it may be hard to determine exactly what lamps and fixtures originally lit your home. Unlike paint colors or wallpaper, you can't chip away layers to find samples of original lighting. Visiting museums

and living history villages, touring restored homes, and thumbing through catalogs of antique and reproduction lighting will help you learn what was available during a particular era.

Early light

If your house dates back to the Colonial period, it would have been lit by fireplaces, candles, and crude smoky lamps, all of which would encourage you to go to bed early. Popular lamps, such as the ''Betty'' and the ''Phoebe,'' consisted of shallow, lidded vessels which the user filled with tallow, grease, or oil. The wick protruded from a small spout and the lamp itself often hung from a hook and chain or stood on a small stand. Most original versions of these lamps have already been snapped up by museums and collectors, but reproductions are widely available as accent accessories.

Simple wrought-iron and tin chandeliers and pierced tin ''Paul Revere'' lanterns with real or electric candles can light a Colonial entry, dining area, or hall.

Multi-candle crystal chandeliers imported from Europe graced upper-class houses. Mirrored wall sconces that reflected and multiplied the light of a single candle also enhanced formal rooms of this period. Reproduction sconces are available in both electrified and nonelectrified versions.

During the first half of the nineteenth century, pewter, tin, and glass whale-oil lamps lit the homes of middle-class families. As lamp technology advanced, models like the Argand, Solar, and Astral combined better draft with circular wicks for brighter light. The first two types featured simple long or bulbous glass chim-

neys attached to brass or bronze Grecian-style column bases. Astrals were capped with more ornate glass shades, often rimmed with dangling crystals.

By the middle of the nineteenth century, kerosene became the fuel of choice. Simple clear glass chimney lamps were mass produced, and you can find originals today at antique shops and flea markets.

In sitting rooms, double-globed oil or kerosene lamps embellished with painted floral designs set a formal decorative tone. Today, these 1880s lamps are often referred to as ''Gone With the Wind'' lamps because they were featured prominently (though historically inaccurately) in the film.

Ladies of the late Victorian period spent many an hour creating ornate pleated silk or cut paper shades bedecked with fringes, ribbons, and glass beadwork, like the reproduction pictured *opposite, left*. This one features a leaded glass center; others let light shine through embroidered and lace panels.

In big cities in the late 1800s, gas-fueled street lighting paved the way for interior gas chandeliers and bracket lights. Because gas burns much brighter than kerosene, frosted or colored glass shades were used to cut glare. Gas fixtures had to be stationary, so a Victorian home usually continued to have oil or kerosene parlor lamps as well as gas fixtures.

Gas lines are often still intact in many houses of this period. If you'd like to have functioning

gaslights, check with your local utility company and discuss code requirements, then have the lines examined for tightness, pressure, and proper cutoff valves. Several manufacturers also make old-fashioned gas street lamps that look right at home in front of a city row house.

By the turn of the century, electric lighting made its home debut. Frequent power failures made combination gas/electric fixtures, such as the polished brass reproduction version shown *opposite, right,* practical, as well as attractive.

Turn-of-the-century leaded glass lamps, such as those of Louis Comfort Tiffany, used electric bulbs, as did Art Deco lamps and fixtures that feature geometric cut-glass frosted shades. Although Tiffany originals are extremely costly, reproductions abound, and originals by less-well-known designers are readily available in antique and secondhand stores.

Putting things in the right light

If you decide to use electrified versions of early lamps and fixtures, or early electric originals, choose bulb sizes and types carefully to approximate the lower illumination levels of earlier kinds of lighting. Several smaller electric fixtures rather than one large one will often give you a closer approximation of the look of oil or gas light. Dimmer switches help you create subtle lighting effects.

In areas such as the kitchen where you need bright task lighting, simple modern fixtures that blend unobtrusively with your decor are often the best options.

INTERIOR DETAILS

Architectural details have a lot to do with why people fall in love with old houses. For many owners, hardwood moldings, plaster ornamentation, and hand-carved mantels justify much of the hard work that goes into renewing an older home.

Some of a home's most glorious assets may be hidden under layers of paint that mask details, or obscured by dirt, grime, wax, and darkened varnish. Cleaning and/or stripping take lots of time and patience, but you'll be inspired by each small area that you finish.

Interior trim may also suffer from more serious neglect. Wooden parts may be rotted, cracked, or missing, and plaster decoration chipped. This means you'll have to fill in the gaps. Start your search for replacements right in your own house. A previous owner may have removed details and stashed them in the attic, basement, garage, or barn. Or maybe you can take parts from an infrequently used room and install them in more public areas.

If your own house doesn't provide what you need, another old house might. Visits to architectural salvage dealers and house wreckers may turn up the missing parts, but be prepared to hunt through an often disorganized jumble of miscellaneous items. Go armed with a list of precise measurements to ensure that what you bring home will fit. Your chances of finding exact duplicates of what you have at home are slim, but if you're looking to replace a whole wall's worth of molding or a set of stair balusters, you may be able to find an appropriate design.

If you're looking for a single item, such as a fretwork spandrel for a doorway that doesn't

New gingerbread and fretwork, like the spider web and other details shown opposite, can be ordered by mail or from local suppliers.

Pressed metal ceiling panels and crown molding, shown above, attach to furring strips. More about pressed metal on page 107.

It's worth a trip to a salvage dealer to search for a mantel for an older home. You'll find a wide variety of designs and materials, such

as the marble and wood examples pictured above, in sizes and proportions likely to correspond to your own fireplace.

have one, matching won't be a problem, and you can simply choose something you like that fits the space.

As good as old

Many firms now specialize in new woodwork, trim, and plaster in authentic old designs. Installing new stock molding or a precast plaster rosette, for example, may be easier than trying to restore badly damaged original trim. Often you can construct a seemingly complicated pattern by layering several pieces of stock molding or trim together.

New woodwork, such as the fretwork shown *opposite,* is usually made of pine, spruce, or redwood rather than fine hardwoods, but you can stain, grain, or paint it to match other trim in your house.

You'll also find specialty catalogs of moldings and trim made of urethane. (For an example, see the cornice pictured on page 140.) The designs are cast from documented wood, marble, and plaster originals and primed to receive either paint or stain. These modern materials are flexible, lightweight, and can be installed with mastic. Applied at the tops of walls or on ceilings, they're hard to tell from the real thing and easy for do-it-yourselfers to use.

In the old days, wood and plaster ornamentation was handmade, often right on site. You, too, can try your hand at doing it the old-fashioned way, but be warned: It took *skilled* craftsmen and their apprentices years to develop these techniques, and you'll have to be willing to invest quite a bit of time to master them yourself. The box at right explains what's involved in duplicating plaster ornamentation. To learn about re-creating wood moldings, see page 136.

To learn about re-creating wood moldings, see page 136.

DUPLICATING PLASTER WORK

Straight runs of plaster molding originally were shaped in place by a craftsman who ran a template across built-up wet plaster. If you live in an area where a lot of restoration is going on, you may be able to find a plasterer who can do this today.

An alternative is to run the molding yourself in sections on a table and then install it in place. To shape the molding, you cut a reverse template from sheet metal backed with wood. Next, attach the template to a jig and run it across layers of wet plaster until the molding is built up to the proper depth.

Ornate plaster decorations get their fine detailing from casting. If you have some original plasterwork intact, use it as a model for a latex rubber mold, which you then fill with wet plaster. You can cast a small mold in place; however, for larger pieces, remove the model from the wall or ceiling and cast the replica on a table. Exact techniques vary, but the basic procedure involves coating the model with several layers of latex rubber to form a flexible casting mold. The rubber mold is then supported for casting by a shell made of plaster, with burlap or cheesecloth embedded for strength.

RE-CREATING WOOD MOLDINGS

Yesteryear's carpenter carried with him a collection of about 50 different molding planes to shape a home's trim. The planes consist of smooth wooden soles from which cutting blades project. Each pass of the plane across a board gradually contours it into the finished molding shape.

Finding old planes takes about as much effort as learning to use them correctly. Auctions, antique dealers, and perhaps some lucky rummaging through barns and attics may turn up some original old planes. You also can find newly manufactured planes in a limited number of styles.

If you have a well-equipped home woodworking shop, you can cut some simple shapes with a router and multiplane. Another option is to attach a special molding-cutter head to your table saw. Like its predecessor, the molding plane, this device can be fitted with about 50 different blades.

Either of these options takes good carpentry skills. If yours aren't up to par, a custom woodworking shop can mill new molding to match a sample of the old, but be prepared to pay a hefty price for the work.

Because it is exposed to the elements, exterior detailing often suffers even more over the years than does interior trim. If you seek to preserve as much of your home's past as possible, you'll probably have to replace missing parts and repair and restore what's left.

Wood ornamentation is especially vulnerable. Start an exterior renewal project by identifying sections of trim that are loose, rotted, or gone. Secure loose sections with long wood screws inserted in pre-drilled pilot holes. Chip out small areas of rot and fill them with wood filler or putty.

If parts are missing, search the premises for pieces that may have been removed and stored. Neighboring homes under demolition and home wrecking and salvage companies also may yield the parts you need.

If you can't find old items, you may need to counterfeit new ones. Moldings, as the box at left explains, may have to be professionally re-created. Sawn-wood trim is a different story. Although it looks lavish, sawn-wood originally was a way to embellish a house when the homeowner could not afford turned or carved ornamentation. Local carpenters cut the trim right on the building site, using designs from popular pattern books or their own imaginations.

You can do the same yourself fairly easily with a jigsaw or saber saw and an electric drill. Often what appears to be an ornate and complicated pattern really is a combination of several simple designs sandwiched together.

Or, if you prefer, you can purchase new reproduction running trim, appliqués, brackets, and corbels, such as the

solid pine examples that are pictured *above*.

Good-bye, old paint

Even ornamentation that is otherwise in good condition may be obscured by too many layers of peeling paint. Most exterior trim was meant to be painted, so preparing it for a new finish is not as painstaking a process as readying interior trim for a natural finish. You'll usually only have to scrape or strip off enough old paint to leave a smooth surface for a new coat to adhere to. An electric paint remover, a flat, heated metal tool that you hold against a painted surface, can help soften old paint for scraping. Some renewers prefer to

burn off exterior paint with a propane torch fitted with a spreader tip, but this tactic can scorch or set fire to old dried-out wood.

Where old paint is tight, smooth, and not too thick, simply wash the surface with a strong trisodium phosphate (TSP) solution and let it dry before painting.

Windows

Old windows with broken panes, rotted sills, and sticking sashes may seem to cry out for total replacement, but first consider repairing them. Windows form an integral part of your home's facade, and changing them can destroy the architectural integrity of the house. In addition, window openings in older homes are usually too large for standard modern windows. If you close in the openings, you sacrifice the original proportions. Also, much of the money you'd save by using standard windows will be spent on carpentry or masonry work to make the openings smaller.

Salvage damaged wood in frames and sills with wood preservatives and putty; broken sash cords can be inexpensively replaced.

If the windows are truly beyond repair, consider custom-made replacements that duplicate the originals as closely as possible. If no original windows remain, do some research to determine the appropriate style. You may immediately think of multipaned windows, like those shown *at right,* but they're only correct for certain periods. Colonial windows featured small panes—often 12 per sash— because glass was hand-blown. As technology advanced, it was possible to make larger panes, and houses were designed with only one or two panes per sash. These simpler windows were often embellished with ornamental casings, lintels, and caps. Many Victorian homes feature hybrids, with multipane top sashes—sometimes incorporating a stained or leaded glass panel—and single-pane bottom sashes.

Storm windows and screens pose a special problem. Old-fashioned wood storms and screens rarely fit as tightly as new metal combination units, must be exchanged twice a year, and require periodic repainting. If you decide to install new combination units, shop for a style and color that will be as unobtrusive as possible.

WOOD FLOORS

Whether you're restoring to period authenticity or updating your home's interior, one thing you'll almost certainly want to preserve is a fine old wood floor. Well-finished wood contributes warmth and style to any decor.

Houses dating back to the Colonial period usually have pine plank floors. Homes of a later vintage feature strip or parquet flooring made of hardwoods such as oak, maple, walnut, teak, and rosewood. You also may find other species of wood, especially those indigenous to your region.

You may not be able to tell much about your wood floors right away. Often previous owners have covered them with linoleum, tile, or carpeting, and your first job will be removing these materials to expose the wood below. Over the years, even uncovered old wood floors may have become dull, dirty, and coated with layers of gummy wax, shellac, and varnish.

Sound footing

You'll probably also face varying degrees of structural damage, including loose boards, squeaks, cracks, warping, rotted or missing lumber, sagging and deteriorated subflooring, joists, or supporting posts.

Your first order of business is to ensure that the floor itself is stable. You may need to strengthen or entirely replace weak supporting members or jack up a sagging floor.

If your floor has minor flaws such as cracks or small gaps, you have several repair options. Fill small cracks with flexible weather stripping, a mixture of sawdust and glue, or sawdust and penetrating sealer. For larger gaps, you can piece in wooden splines stained to match. Use wood or cork plugs to fill holes.

Badly damaged parts of the floor will need to be replaced, and finding new wood to match the old can pose quite a challenge. Your best bet may be to cut out pieces from a closet or other concealed spot and use them to make repairs in highly visible areas. Some firms specialize in salvaging lumber from old buildings; these firms may be good sources if you're dealing with a very old floor.

You also can buy new wood of the same species and experiment with stains to blend the patch in. Have the new boards custom-milled to fit, or, if you have the skills and equipment, save money by planing and cutting them yourself. Because lumber dimensions have changed over the years, the widths of standard modern precut flooring won't fit into an old floor. Also, most old flooring is thicker than its modern counterparts, so you'll often have to shim up the patch to make the floor level.

New wood floors

If the original wood floor is in poor condition, or if you don't have wood flooring at all, you have a variety of options. Oak strips laid in a horizontal, diagonal, or herringbone pattern make a simple and relatively economical choice. New pine boards or planks, either clear-finished or painted, provide an appropriate background for a country-style or Colonial room.

For more elegant interiors, do-it-yourselfers can install hardwood parquet tiles. Fine decorative hardwood borders, such as the teak strips shown *opposite,* can enhance an inlaid carpet or surround a plainer wood central section.

SCRUB, SAND, OR STRIP?

Even if a floor is sound, you will almost certainly have to refresh its surface. First, try thoroughly cleaning and renewing the old finish on a small area of the floor. Scrub with mineral spirits or turpentine and fine steel wool, and wipe dry with paper towels. Or scrub with a stiff brush and detergent, rinse, and let dry, then rub with mineral spirits. These methods will remove dirt and built-up wax, and the finish may look bright again as is, or need only a coat of new sealer or finish.

If cleaning doesn't suffice, you'll have to remove the old finish. You can do this by sanding off the old finish with a machine or stripping it with chemicals. Sanding removes about $1/16$ inch of the flooring, and leaves a smooth, regular surface. Stripping removes only the old finish, leaving much more of the floor's original character intact.

Before deciding which method to use, think about how you'd like the finished floor to look. Do you want to retain some of the patina, irregularities, and character of the original, or would you prefer an old floor that looks brand new? Also consider the wood itself. Sanding may be too harsh for soft pine floors, delicate parquets, or any wood that's been thinned by previous sandings.

Stripping means a lot of downtime—down on your hands and knees with scrapers and steel wool. If you're dealing with a relatively small area, the results may be worth the effort, but stripping a very large area is often not practical. On the other hand, you can strip a small area at a time and contain the mess. Stripping will raise the wood grain, so some sanding will be required before applying the new finish.

Most professional refinishers sand floors with power machinery; you can rent sanders and do the work yourself, but be prepared for a job that requires a lot of muscle and creates quite a mess. A drum sander is heavy, and you have to be strong enough to control it. Otherwise you risk gouging and damaging your floors. You'll also need to wear a dust mask and turn off any pilot lights because the dust is highly flammable.

Whether you hire someone or do the work yourself, sanding usually involves three passes with gradually finer grades of sandpaper. After sanding, the floor is vacuumed and wiped with a tack cloth to remove all traces of dust. Next, a stain is applied—if you want one—followed by a sealer and a clear finish.

HANDPRINTED FOR THE CAMRON · STANFORD HOUSE

Many chapters of a home's history are written on its walls. Carefully peel back layers of wallpaper or chip off generations of paint, and you'll often be able to read a home's decorating story. You may not want to duplicate what you find, but you'll get an idea of color schemes, patterns, and scales of designs used in earlier days.

If you're interested in creating an authentic period interior, combine what you learn from your own walls with other research. Browse through historical museums, preservation society journals, library collections, restored villages and homes, and specialty catalogs.

Some wallpaper and paint manufacturers offer documented collections of historic colors and designs that are accurate reproductions of original wallpaper or paint samples. Other companies sell patterns and colors more loosely modeled on ones known to have been used during a particular period. You'll find a variety of styles and materials to choose from when you shop.

Paint
Just as it is today, painting was a practical and economical decorating alternative in earlier times. The walls of a small Colonial farmhouse, for example, typically were coated with whitewash or painted with pigments mixed in oil or milk. Prior to the mid-1800s, when color printing machines came to America, wallpaper was imported from Europe and too costly for many families. Even in wealthier homes, or homes from later periods, walls might be a combination of painted surfaces and wallpaper borders or panels.

Several firms still produce milk paints, and most major paint manufacturers offer authentic color collections in both latex and alkyd.

Be on the lookout for a finish called calcimine. Calcimine is a wash, not a true paint, that was popular from the 1700s to the early 1900s. Made from clear glue, whiting, water, and sometimes a tint, calcimine was an attractive, economical way to achieve a flat, silky finish on plaster walls. Repainting meant washing off the original coat and applying a new one. If you like the look, you may want to continue using calcimine, but because it's water soluble, it's difficult to maintain in high-use areas.

Latex paint will not adhere to calcimined walls. You need to wash off the calcimine with water and trisodium phosphate (TSP) before priming and painting. Oil-based paints will cover calcimine, but over the years they may start to peel. If you're faced with this situation, you'll have to steam off the oil paint, then wash off the calcimine underneath.

Wallpaper
A few wallpaper firms carry original old papers, and others will custom-reproduce papers for you from a small sample— but both of these options are extremely expensive. You can find authentic reproduction wallpapers or modern designs with a similar flavor to suit nearly any historic period. Some designs, such as the ones shown *opposite*, are hand-screened the old-fashioned way. The paper on the wall features a willow pattern derived from an original designed by William Morris in 1874; the other is an Eastlake frieze with a Japanese motif. If you're decorating on a limited budget, machine-printed versions are more economical.

Stenciling
Stenciling was the poor man's wallpaper in Colonial days. Designs inspired by wallpaper patterns often covered entire walls, and more modest stenciled borders simulated moldings and chair rails.

Mass-produced affordable wallpaper replaced stenciling as an overall wall treatment, but the Victorians continued to use stenciling to accent architectural features and in conjunction with other wall treatments. A typical wall might feature a stenciled border above the wainscoting, wallpaper above that, topped with a stenciled frieze below the ceiling molding.

You can design your own stencils, basing them on motifs from wallpaper, fabric, old quilts, or books of traditional patterns—or purchase ready-cut stencil kits from museums and craft shops.

Paneling
Restoring fine old wood wainscoting or paneling is well worth the effort. You may be able to clean and revive woodwork that's merely dirty or dulled by layers of wax and shellac or varnish without resorting to stripping. Page 138 explains how.

The inexpensive soft wood used to trim many homes was meant to be painted or artificially grained to imitate hardwood. Before you start a wholesale stripping operation, scrape away a small area in an unobtrusive place to determine whether the wood is attractive enough to warrant a natural finish.

If your home doesn't have decorative woodwork, you can purchase new, old-style paneled wainscoting, although it's quite expensive. Or you may be able to find salvaged panels, as shown *opposite*.

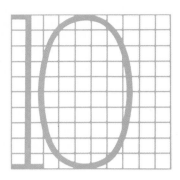

FINISHING AND FURNISHING

A renewed house isn't a cake which is baked and then just "decorated." The same clear vision of the future that you need to see a restoration or rehabilitation project through to its completion is equally important when it comes to integrating building and remodeling plans with decorating details. From the moment you start work, you must cultivate an image in your mind's eye of what you want the interior to be like. Function and good looks should go together in a happy blend of beauty, practicality, and your personal style. This chapter will give you a start toward creating that blend.

PLANNING ROOM ARRANGEMENTS

Because an older home is likely to be far less standardized than a newer one, finishing and furnishing a renewed house poses some special challenges. You must deal with unusual architectural features, both good and bad; you may encounter measurements and proportions that do not conform to contemporary standards; and, perhaps most important, you need to decide exactly how much of the past you want to live with.

Start, not by compiling lists of specific furnishings, but rather by considering the *function* of each room or zone. Just because a space is labeled "dining room" doesn't mean you must furnish it that way. If formal dining is not a family priority, perhaps the room would be better used as a combination dining room/den—a transformation easily accomplished by good furniture selection and placement.

Your choice of furnishings and their arrangement also can alter the sense of space in a room. For example, a large room, particularly one with formal moldings and grand-scale windows, may seem cold and austere if furnishings are arranged in one massive grouping. Two or three cozier areas will make the large space more workable.

Consider experimenting with the shapes of your groupings, too. For instance, diagonal arrangements often make a square room function in a less formal and more conversation-oriented way. Also think of arranging furnishings to focus on a special view or architectural feature—something you're likely to have plenty of in a renewed home.

Now analyze the logical traffic patterns into, out of, and through each of your rooms. For instance, must you walk through the living room to reach a dining room or patio? If so, your proposed room arrangement should take this into account.

Getting it all to fit
To get an accurate sense of exactly where furnishings should go, and what sizes and shapes would work best, measure each room and sketch it out on a piece of graph paper, using one square to equal one square foot of floor space. Indicate doorways, the direction in which doors swing, windows, and other architectural features. After you've graphed it all out, but before you buy the furnishings, you might want to make full-scale paper cutouts of the pieces you plan to purchase, then double-check your plans on the floors of the rooms themselves, as illustrated in the photo *opposite*.

How do you envision the completed project?
Once you have a good idea about how you're going to use your home's space, you're ready to consider specific furnishings.

If you plan to furnish your home in more or less "period" style, you've probably been careful to avoid decidedly modern cabinet hardware or other details that will clash with the mood you want to create. On the other hand, if you plan to furnish a renewed home with sleek contemporary furnishings or a combination of several styles, you have more flexibility in choosing architectural accessories such as hardware and millwork, as well as the furnishings themselves. The following pages show three renewed homes that have been finished and furnished with three distinctly different approaches.

A RESTORED HOUSE

One of the most exciting things about the spread of "restoration fever" is its energizing effect on big cities and small towns throughout the country. Entire neighborhoods, once run-down and all-but-forgotten, are springing back to life as homeowners adapt their old houses to modern-day living. If your renewed home is located in a restoration district, you'll probably make every effort to return the exterior, in scrupulous detail, to its original period grandeur. But what about the inside? Must it, too, be a reflection of the age in which the house was built, or can you creatively combine the best of furnishings from a variety of periods?

The handsome Columbus, Georgia, home pictured here and on the following two pages is part of a neighborhood that was considered a slum at the time the owners purchased it. Examine the view from the street, pictured *above,* and you can see that careful attention to structural detail, along with an authentic yellow-and-white exterior, has restored this house to how it looked 100 years ago—and also put it in harmony with the appearance of neighboring homes.

At first glance, the interior also may seem to be faithful to the Victorian era, and some of its elements are. But the owners chose to borrow styles and furnishings from earlier times as well.

The dining room shown *opposite,* for example, is elegantly furnished with eighteenth-century pieces

whose designs predate the Victorian home by a century or more.

The living room, visible in the background of the photo, also is furnished with a mix of centuries-old designs—an eighteenth-century camelback sofa and an even earlier William and Mary-style armchair.

Other elements of the interior were restored to their former glory. Chipped and cracked old plaster came off and the walls were resurfaced; the plank floors, formerly under layers of linoleum and carpeting, were exposed, scraped, and refinished; and many latter-day room partitions were torn out. This dining room, for instance, had been turned into a kitchen many years ago.

After the partitions were removed and the rooms put

back to their original uses, new paint was used to emphasize the delightful old millwork.

Choose furnishings you can live with

Many owners of restored homes, especially those located in historic districts such as this one, insist that nearly every element be finished and furnished as it might have been when the home was built. But before you decide to go this route, consider whether you really *want* to live almost exactly as our ancestors did. A circa-1880 house, for instance, doesn't have to have rooms full of Victorian carvings and horsehair upholstery fabrics, although a few such accents may heighten its charm. You may even want a sprinkling of contemporary furnishings in your restored home.

(continued)

A RESTORED HOUSE
(continued)

Almost no one would want to live in a home with a kitchen from the distant past. However, if you're faced with this situation, you have two choices: Forget entirely about authenticity, add a modern-day facility, and visually separate it from other living areas; or blend up-to-date fixtures, appliances, and surfaces into a period setting.

The kitchen in the house featured here takes the latter approach. As you can see in the photo *at right,* it was redone in a grand style befitting the gracious Victorian ambience of the rest of the home—but outfitted with every contemporary cooking convenience.

The focal point of the new kitchen is a functional island, dressed up with an ornately carved canopy that adds special charm without interfering with efficiency. The trim consists of old posts and accessory pieces salvaged from the porch of a neighboring home that was beyond repair and had to be demolished.

In contrast to the remodeled kitchen, the entry hall pictured *opposite* was rebuilt in all its original grandeur. The dado was painted gray to highlight the decades-old chair rails and baseboards. A Victorian hall tree, colorful leaded-glass windows, and antique gaslights now wired for electricity combine the charm of the 1880s with the safety and efficiency of the 1980s.

Determining your home's original interior design
As part of your restoration project, you may be eager to find out as much as possible about how your home's interior was furnished. Old photographs may help. Although

interior photographs are next to impossible to find, an exterior photograph may reveal a precious glimpse of an original window treatment, for example.

If your house was built in this century and you're lucky enough to find an elderly former resident or perhaps an older neighbor who remembers being inside the house decades ago, you may have a direct source of information about the types of furnishings and colors that were used when the home was young.

Learn about the period
If you can't get information about your house, or if you would like to supplement it, look for books in the local library or get in touch with historic preservation groups. It may be worth your while to investigate mail-order catalogs of the period, too, to determine the types of furnishings that were commonly sold. Also visit local museums and find out whether any other restored homes in your area are open for public tours. Many local preservation groups sponsor annual walking tours of faithfully restored neighborhoods and homes.

Local antique dealers and auctioneers also are excellent sources of information about furnishing styles and periods. Once you've settled on the types of pieces you want, they'll also be able to help you locate them.

Don't overlook fine furniture reproductions
When it comes to furnishing your home, don't overlook the wealth of high-quality reproduction case goods and uphol-

stered furnishings now on the market. These range from simple country-style items to richly detailed designs dating from the 1700s and 1800s.

A number of museums and large-scale restoration projects, including the Museum of American Folk Art (located in New York City), Delaware's Winterthur Museum (which features fine eighteenth-century furnishings), and Colonial Williamsburg, have sponsored

collections of reproductions that are faithful in every detail to the originals.

Whether you select genuine antique furnishings or reproductions, you still need to provide for modern-day accompaniments. Television sets and stereo gear, for example, can be neatly hidden in old chests or armoires.

FINISHING AND FURNISHING

A RENOVATED HOUSE

Renovating falls into the broad middle ground between restoring a house and remodeling one from stem to stern. In a renovated house, your range of finishing and furnishing options is equally broad. Unless your house has particular historical significance, an eclectic approach might well be the one to take. Eclecticism gives you the freedom to mix the best of old and new furnishings and architectural details for a result that's as personal as it is livable.

Eclectic decorating is not merely an excuse for haphazardly mixing unrelated items. Instead, an eclectic scheme carefully assembles the best items from different periods or styles. When you're renewing an old house, eclecticism means you can keep what you like—and put aside the rest.

Save the best architectural details

When you're the proud owner of an older home, like the stately 1920s Colonial Revival house featured here, treat it carefully. If your style is eclectic, do a little research to avoid unwittingly destroying important architectural details.

Even if you decide to decorate with a modern bent inside, it's usually best to preserve many of the home's exterior features. Old windows and doors, such as the pediment-style entryway shown *above,* for example, are almost always worth saving.

The solarium of this house, pictured *at left,* demonstrates how successfully old architecture and new furnishings can be mixed. The charming mullioned windows are vital to the charm of the room. But the way the room is decorated brings it into the easygoing twentieth-century style. Covered with slick white paint, the old window frames and walls team with new wood floors to provide a sleek background for an interesting mix of furnishings. Contemporary seating pieces and tables blend into the background, allowing rugs and a whimsical, ceiling-hung kite to brighten the color scheme.

Do an architectural survey of your home

Take stock of the architectural features of your own home. Are doors and window trim especially attractive? If so, consider refinishing them or highlighting them with a coat of paint to contrast with the walls. Think at least twice, though, before painting any fine old interior wood details; the grain and natural finish may be more desirable than any decorative effect you could achieve through painting. If the woodwork is nondescript, simply paint it to match the walls.

What about the flooring? Are your wood floors in good shape and worth refinishing? That's often the case in well-built older homes. In bathrooms, old tile floors are a consideration, too. Are they attractive—or just cracked and dated? If they don't suit your style, don't feel guilty about recovering them.

(continued)

149

A RENOVATED HOUSE
(continued)

When you're deciding what to save and what to discard in an eclectic scheme, also consider built-in features. Structural details such as carved stair rails, bookcases, fireplaces, and buffets are often charming and probably worth saving. If you're not sure about the age or significance of these details, a little library research can inform you.

Your survey also should include smaller details, such as light fixtures. You may want to save especially attractive or valuable old ceiling fixtures, but many are just plain out of date. Replace these with new hanging fixtures or track lights. Save the old fixtures you remove, however, in case future owners of the house want to reinstall them.

Update with livability in mind
The home shown here and on the previous two pages offers other adaptable ideas for creating an eclectic scheme.

At the back of the house, the living room pictured *opposite* was dark and closed-in before the homeowners began their update. A new sliding glass door opens out to a new backyard deck, leaving the home's street-side appearance unchanged.

As you see here, contemporary furnishings can settle easily into an older home. In this living room, for example, white paint brightens the walls and provides a background for dramatic contemporary furnishings. Interesting wooden ceiling moldings were retained but also painted white. The owners also replaced an outmoded and inefficient chandelier with new track lighting.

A juxtaposition of furniture and architectural styles often adds vitality to both the old

and the new. Charming architectural details, such as old wood-plank floors and fine woodwork, can add subtle character to your decorating scheme. And a few simple, contemporary pieces of furniture can make a formal older home much more compatible with the life-styles of today's families.

Nooks and crannies
Old-house attics, which often have high enough rooflines to be used without structural remodeling, offer their own brand of charm. In the attic shown *at upper right,* white-painted walls keep the bedroom light and airy. New furnishings offer modern appeal and function. An old-fashioned dormer window (not shown) reminds you that this is an older house. Carpeted floors minimize noise when the children play upstairs.

Two stories below, the outmoded kitchen also was remodeled. Now a sleek, functional galley, the kitchen boasts a small breakfast nook with a new fireplace and sliding glass door, shown *at lower right.* A trestle table and hoopback chairs are not only easy to care for and very comfortable, but also fit in nicely with the original, well-cared-for oak floors.

Making a mixture into a blend
When you mix furnishing styles, use color to tie unrelated items together. In this home, neutrals and bright primary colors are the unifying force. Another unifier is mood. Most furnishings are basically formal or informal, and pieces that share a mood often go well together even when their ages are centuries apart.

A REMODELED HOUSE

A house doesn't have to be ancient to benefit from renewing. Even though its exterior and systems may be up to date, the interior layout and decor may badly need refreshment, if not a total overhaul. If you have a middle-aged ranch house with everything but charm, remodel it beautifully—and on a budget—using new finishes and furnishings. Here and on the following pages, we'll show you how one family transformed a typical 1950s tract house into their dream home.

The exterior of the suburban home pictured on these pages typifies the subdivision style of a generation ago. The present owners were attracted by its quiet and convenient location, access to an excellent school system, a moderate price tag, pleasantly "grown-in" landscaping, and structural soundness. Best of all, they realized that the home had all the square footage they needed—space they knew they could face-lift to suit their streamlined style of living.

Open things up

Small, chopped-up rooms were a problem, but the family found they could give the aging house the openness, livability, and up-to-date styling of a 1980s home without major reconstruction.

The update began with removal of a non-supporting wall between the dining room and the living room pictured *at left*. The once-cramped living areas both feel larger now and also benefit by sharing a wealth of incoming light from their once-separated windows.

Once the structural changes were made, the homeowners relied on decorating strategies to complete the rejuvenation of their home. The decorating began with a coat of fresh white paint on the walls, ceiling, woodwork, doors, even the aluminum window trim.

White window shades in some rooms and blinds in others, such as the living room featured here, provide privacy and continue the all-important flow of space and light. The white vertical blinds add an illusion of height to the rooms and disguise the lines of the old windows. These blinds offer an additional bonus by creating a contemporary, floor-to-ceiling "window-wall" effect.

The next major decorative change came with a new floor of off-white Italian tile, chosen both for its cool, contemporary look and for its resistance to the wear and tear of daily family life. The owners had the tile professionally installed; however, to save money, they did the grouting themselves.

(continued)

153

A REMODELED HOUSE
(continued)

The most successful remodelings are those in which one room flows cohesively into another. A smooth transition is easy to achieve if you employ similar (or matching) materials and colors throughout your home to provide visual links from one area to the next.

The photo *above*, which shows the view from the back door toward the living and dining areas, illustrates how two elements—the white-painted walls and the floor tiles—provide the needed visual tie in this home. White "makeup" also gives the home a surpris-ingly expansive quality that belies its modest dimensions.

The photo here also shows the importance of looking after every detail when you're refurbishing a house. The dated galley kitchen in this home, for instance, could have ruined the effect of the other cosmetic touches had it not been facelifted, too.

Old cabinets and worn countertops were a surefire tip-off to the home's age, but a bit of elbow grease solved the problem without any major investment. The old cabinets—cleaned and sanded—now sport a sleek coating of white enamel. New countertops match the new snack bar and complete the update.

Finally, furnishings

Furnishings play a vital role in any home. To achieve the architectural mood they wanted, the owners of this home opted for a mix of new, moderately priced pieces. Modular, solid-foam seating pieces are budget-priced, yet their low profiles and clean lines suit the family's sophisticated tastes. These modular units are especially practical, since they fold out for guest sleeping.

For chic dining, Breuer chairs team with a handsome Parsons table. The table was purchased at an unfinished-furniture store, then given a high-style treatment of plastic laminate.

To provide storage space without overpowering the small home, the owners relied on homemade wall-hung shelves. The shelves, made of inexpensive fiberboard and painted a warm wheat color, make good use of a sliver of wall space, yet their open design is light and airy. The adjustable shelves hold books, stereo gear, and a portable TV set.

RENEWING AN OLD HOUSE

WHERE TO GO FOR MORE INFORMATION

Better Homes and Gardens® Books

If you'd like to learn more about renewing older homes, these Better Homes and Gardens® books can help.

Better Homes and Gardens®
NEW DECORATING BOOK
How to translate ideas into workable solutions for every room in your home. Choosing a style, furniture arrangements, windows, walls and ceilings, floors, lighting, and accessories. 433 color photos, 76 how-to illustrations, 432 pages.

Better Homes and Gardens®
COMPLETE GUIDE TO HOME REPAIR,
MAINTENANCE, & IMPROVEMENT
Inside your home, outside your home, your home's systems, basics you should know. Anatomy and step-by-step drawings illustrate components, tools, techniques, and finishes. 515 how-to techniques; 75 charts; 2,734 illustrations; 552 pages.

Better Homes and Gardens®
COMPLETE GUIDE TO GARDENING
A comprehensive guide for beginners and experienced gardeners. Houseplants, lawns and landscaping, trees and shrubs, greenhouses, insects and diseases. 461 color photos, 434 how-to illustrations, 37 charts, 552 pages.

Better Homes and Gardens®
STEP-BY-STEP BUILDING SERIES
A series of do-it-yourself building books that provides step-by-step illustrations and how-to information for starting and finishing many common construction projects and repair jobs around your house. More than 90 projects and 1,200 illustrations in this series of six 96-page books:
STEP-BY-STEP BASIC PLUMBING
STEP-BY-STEP BASIC WIRING
STEP-BY-STEP BASIC CARPENTRY
STEP-BY-STEP HOUSEHOLD REPAIRS
STEP-BY-STEP MASONRY & CONCRETE
STEP-BY-STEP CABINETS & SHELVES

Additional Books

The following books are just a sampling of the many that offer advice for those thinking about renewing; how-to-do-it guidelines for those who are undertaking the task; and periodically reviewed and updated lists of suppliers for those who need authentic or specialized materials.

Organizing for Historic Preservation: A Resource Guide.
New Haven, CT: Connecticut Trust for Historic Preservation, 1983. A 48-page pamphlet of advice from preservation experts.

The American House, by Mary Mix Foley. New York: Harper and Row, 1980. An illustrated guide to house styles.

The Third Old House Catalog, compiled by Lawrence Grow. New York: Macmillan (Collier Books), 1982. Annotated listing of supplies of products and services—from cornices to dampers to furniture, and much more. Also extensive book list.

Preserving and Maintaining the Older Home, by Shirley Hanson and Nancy Hubby. New York: McGraw-Hill, 1983. Good general information for homeowners.

So You Want to Fix Up an Old House, by Peter Hotton. Boston: Little, Brown, 1979. Background reading; practical information.

Restoring Old Houses, by Nigel Hutchins. New York: Van Nostrand Reinhold, 1982. Appealing photographs and practical advice.

Old House Woodwork Restoration, by Ed Johnson. Englewood Cliffs, NJ: Prentice-Hall, 1983. Detailed, illustrated do-it-yourself advice.

The Old-House Journal Compendium, edited by Clem Labine and Carolyn Flaherty. Two volumes. Woodstock, NY: The Overlook Press (paperback), 1983. Selected articles from past issues of the magazine.

The Old-House Journal Catalog. 69A Seventh Avenue, Brooklyn, NY. Buyer's guide to products and services; updated annually.

Renovation: A Complete Guide, by Michael Litchfield. New York: John Wiley, 1982. Detailed advice about renewing older homes.

Five Acres and Dementia: How to Restore an Old Texas Farmhouse and Keep Smiling, by Augusta Mutchler. San Antonio: Corona Publishing. Fun to read, with insights into what it's like to get involved in this kind of project.

A Gift to the Street, by Carol Olwell and Judith Lynch Waldhorn. New York: St. Martin's Press, 1976. Victorian architecture in words and photographs.

Respectful Rehabilitation: Answers to Your Questions About Old Buildings. Washington, DC: Preservation Press (publishing branch of the National Trust for Historic Preservation), 1982. Covers both residential and commercial structures.

Complete Guide to Residential Remodeling, by Mortimer P. Reed. Englewood Cliffs, NJ: Prentice-Hall, 1983. Basic advice and how-to.

Renovating the Victorian House: A Guide for Owners and Aficionados of Old Houses, by Katherine Knight Rusk. San Francisco: 101 Productions, 1983. Covers all aspects—structural, decorative, and financial.

American Architecture, by Marcus Whiffen and Frederick Koeper. Volume 1: 1607-1860; Volume 2: 1860-1976. Cambridge, MA.: The MIT Press, 1983. Historical overview.

WHERE TO GO FOR MORE INFORMATION
(continued)

Magazines

These two magazines are excellent sources of advice, information, and good reading.

Historic Preservation. A bimonthly publication of the National Trust for Historic Preservation (see address listing under "Other Sources"). It features articles about successful preservation efforts throughout the nation, as well as an extensive book review section.

The Old-House Journal. 69A Seventh Avenue, Brooklyn, NY 11217. A monthly publication emphasizing do-it-yourself methods for restoring, maintaining, and decorating houses built prior to about 1940.

Other Sources of Information

Many government and private organizations and agencies offer advice for individuals and communities interested in preserving or reviving older homes, commercial structures, and land. These are key sources of information. We have listed only a sampling. You will find municipal and state groups in your area who can give you detailed, specific advice about a project.

Historic House Association of America
1600 H Street NW
Washington, DC 20006

Land Trust Exchange
3 Joy Street
Boston, MA 02108
Compiles a directory of local land conservation organizations; useful for those interested in preserving or renewing agricultural properties.

The National Trust for Historic Preservation
1785 Massachusetts Avenue NW
Washington, DC 20036

U.S. Department of the Interior
Washington, DC 20240
There are two separate sources at the above address.

For information about tax incentives and certification of historic buildings, write to:
Chief of Technical Preservation Services
National Park Service

For general advice and information, write to:
Office of Archaeology and Historic Preservation
Heritage Conservation and Recreation Service

Many companies that produce or distribute specialized renewing materials make their catalogs available to interested consumers. Addresses, descriptive information, and charges, if any, were current at the time this book was printed but may have changed.

Bangkok Industries
1900 S. 20th Street
Philadelphia, PA 19145
(Wood flooring, wainscoting)

Bradbury & Bradbury Wallpapers
Box 155
Benicia, CA 94510
$1.00 (Wall coverings)

Chicago Faucet
2100 S. Nuclear Drive
Des Plaines, IL 60018
(Plumbing hardware)

Cumberland Woodcraft Co.
2500 Walnut Bottom Road
Carlisle, PA 17013
$3.50 (Wood trim)

Focal Point, Inc.
2005 Marietta Road NW
Atlanta, GA 30318
$3.00 (Ceiling coves, cornices, rosettes, plaster-look castings)

W.F. Norman Co.
Box 323
Nevada, MO 64772
$3.00 (Tin ceilings)

The Renovator's Supply
1519 Northfield Road
Millers Falls, MA 01349
$2.00 (Materials for entire renovation, including lighting, hardware, and plumbing fixtures; wall coverings; and more)

Shades of the Past
Box 502
Corte Madera, CA 94925
$3.00 (Lighting, shades, and lamp bases)

Vintage Wood Works
513 S. Adams
Dept. 210
Fredericksburg, TX 78624
$2.00 (Gingerbread, fretwork, corbels, brackets, gazebos)

ACKNOWLEDGMENTS

Architects and Designers

The following is a page-by-page listing of the architects and designers whose work appears in this book.

Cover:
Clare and Werner Sahling
Pages 6-7
Bette Zakarian
Pages 8-9
Clare and Werner Sahling
Page 10
Robert Roscoe
Page 11
Herbert A. Ketcham, AIA
Pages 14-15
Nan Bennett
Pages 16-17
Ben Lloyd
Pages 34-35
Jeremiah Eck
Pages 42-43
Charles O. Griffin,
Englebrecht & Griffin
Pages 66-67
Ben Dooley
Pages 68-69
Sisco/Lubotsky Assoc., Ltd.
Pages 70-71
Robert Roscoe
Pages 72-73
James Bukey
Pages 74-75
John E. Seals
Pages 76-77
Dan Metzler
Pages 78-79
Adelaide Osborne/Cybele Interiors
Pages 80-81
James Pfefferkorn

Pages 82-83
Robert Roscoe
Pages 84-85
Suzanne Moore-Wollum
Page 87
Jim McIlzain
Page 86
Margaret D. Woodring
Page 88-89
Dane Art Metamorphosis
Page 92
Pittsburgh Paint
Page 94
Bob Buckter Color Consultant
Page 97
Robert Roscoe
Pages 98-99
Bob Kirkland, Kirkland/Ogram and Associates, Inc.
Pages 100-101
Sidney Weinberg
Pages 102-103
Bill and Denise Shields
Pages 104-105
Martin & Jones
Page 107
Bob Kirkland, Kirkland/Ogram and Associates, Inc.
Page 109
Ernest Dorfi, AIA
Page 110
Pamela Hughes & Co.
Page 112
Stephen Farrow
Page 113
Historic Savannah Foundation Inc.
Page 116
Michael and Jaye Kephart
Page 117
Jim Burns
Pages 144-147
Lee Bayard
Pages 148-151
Barbara Epstein
Pages 152-155
Tom and Ricki Rosengren

Photographers and Illustrators

We extend our thanks to the following photographers and illustrators whose creative talents and technical skills contributed much to this book.

Pages 20-33
Hedrich-Blessing
Also:
Ernest Braun
Bob Buckter
Ross Chapple
Jim Hedrich/Hedrich-Blessing
Thomas Hooper
Hopkins Associates
William N. Hopkins
Scott Little
Fred Lyon
Maris/Semel
E. Alan McGee
Frank Lotz Miller
Joe Standart
Jessie Walker

Associations and Companies

Our appreciation goes to the following associations and companies for providing both information and materials for this book.

Bangkok Industries
Bradbury & Bradbury Wallpapers
Chicago Faucet
Cumberland Woodcraft Company
Cutler Corporation
Des Moines Public Library
Englebrecht & Griffin
Focal Point, Inc.
W.F. Norman Co.
Nulph Construction
Renovator's Supply
Shades of the Past
Sherman Hill Association, Inc.
United Federal Savings, Des Moines, Iowa
Vintage Wood Works

Page numbers in *italics* refer to illustrations or illustrated text.

A-C

Adding on, *68-69*
  keeping room for granary, 80, *81*
Air conditioning, *119,* 121
Architects, use of, 64-65
Architectural details, 12
  exterior *12-13, 96-97, 136-137*
  interior, *114-115, 134-135*
Architectural features, treatment of, in renovation, 149
Armored cable, 124
Assessor's office, research at, 43
Attic, bedroom in, *150*
Bathroom and kitchen hardware, *131*
Bathrooms, planning for, in renewal, 56
Bathroom window, wood trim for, *117*
Bay windows, detailing around, *95*
Beams
  ceilings, *66-67, 74*
  with skylights, *116*
Bedroom in attic, *150*
Bidding by contractors, 65
Blinds, vertical, *152-153*
Block grant, qualifying for, 83
Boilers in piped heating systems, 120
Brackets as exterior ornamentation, *96, 136*
Brass water supply lines, 128
Breakfast nook, *150*
Brick, use of, in farm-building renewal, *80, 81*
Bump-outs, *90,* 91
BX (armored cable), 124
Cable, electrical, kinds of, 124
Calcimine, 141
Cape Cod Colonial House, *94*
Carpenter Gothic cottage, *32-33*
Cast iron for drain-waste-vent lines, 129

Ceilings
  beamed, *66-67, 74*
  decorative treatments, *106,* 107, *135*
  removal, *73, 99, 107*
Central air conditioning, *119,* 121
Chimney, inspecting, 38
China cupboard, woodwork on, *114*
Close-in house types
  suburban, *28-29*
  Victorian, *26-27*
Colonial-inspired suburban homes, *28-29, 31*
Colonial-period lighting, 133
Color
  for exterior paint, 87, *92-95*
  for restoration, 58-59
Contractors, use of, 65
Conversion of commercial buildings, *14-15,* 24, *78-79*
Cooling systems, *119,* 121
Copper water supply lines, 128
Corbels, *136*
Costs of renewal, 62-63
Crown molding, pressed metal, *135*

D-F

Decks, *90-91*
Department of the Interior, U.S., standards of, 48
Dining/living area in open plan, *78-79*
Dining rooms
  during/after renewal, *16-17*
  in restored houses, *71, 144*
Door hardware, *130,* 131
Doors
  French, *67*
  increased efficiency, need for, 49
  renewal, *111*
Dormers, treatment of, 92
Drain-waste-vent (DWV) lines, 126, *127,* 129
Drawings of house
  professional, kinds of, 54-55
  rough, preparation of, *50-51*
Ducted heating systems, 41, *118-119,* 120

Eastlake frieze (wallpaper pattern), *140*
Eclectic decorating in renovation, *148-151*
Economic Recovery Tax Act of 1981, 75
Electrical systems, 41, *122-123,* 124-125
Electric lighting, early, *132,* 133
Energy considerations, 49, 88
  heating units, 120
Entrance halls in restored houses, *10, 147*
Entryways
  pediment-style, *149*
  shed-roofed, *88-89*
Exposed wiring, 124
Exteriors, renewing, 84-97
  design approaches, 57
  drawings of house, preparation, *50,* 51
  ornamental details, *12-13, 96-97, 136*
  paint, *92-95*
    removing, 136
    for restorations, 87
  renovation
    ranch house, *90-91*
    with roof extension, *88-89*
  restoration, *8-9, 21, 70, 84-87, 145*
  windows, 136-137, *137*
Fabric-covered cable, 124
Farm buildings, renewed, *80-81*
Farmhouses, 32
  exteriors, *7*
    red paint, *92*
    restoration, *84-85*
    Victorian, *34-35*
Faucets, *131*
Fence, wrought-iron, *86*
Financial considerations, 19, 45
  costs, 62-63
  tax incentives, 75
Fireplaces, *102, 112-113*
  in breakfast nook, *150*
  curving, *101*
  walls around, *81*
    as focal points, *68-69, 76-77*
"Fishing" of wires, 124-125

Floors
  tile, Italian, *152, 154*
  wood, 138, *139*
French doors, *67*
Fretwork, *134*
Furnaces, 41, *118,* 119-120
Furnishings, 142-154
  plans, 142, *143*
  remodeled house, *152-154*
  renovated house, *148-151*
  restored house, *144-147*

G-L

Galvanized steel water supply lines, 128
Gas/electric light fixture, *132*
Gaslights, 133
Gas lines, 129
Gazebos, attached, *9, 87*
Georgian town house, *25*
Gingerbread (trim), Queen Anne, *97*
Granary, home from *80-81*
Grants, government, qualifying for, 83
Grounded wiring, 125
Ground fault circuit interrupters (GFCI), 125
Halls, entrance, in restored houses, *10, 147*
Hall tree, Victorian, *147*
Hardware, *130-131*
Heating systems
  ducted, 41, *118-119,* 120
  piped, 49, 120-121
Hot-water heating systems, 120-121
Income-producing properties, tax incentives for, 75
Insect infestation, inspecting for 41,
Interpretive restoration, *10,* 11, 52, 87
Island, kitchen, *146*
Italianate Victorian homes, *21, 27, 95*
Keeping room 80, *81*
Kitchens, *103*
  finishing/furnishing
    in remodeled house, *154*
    in renovated house, *150*
    in restored house, *146*
  living with remodeling, 17
  planning for renewal, 56
  pressed metal ceiling, *106*

Kite, ceiling-hung, *148-149*
Knob-and-tube wiring, 124
Lamps, period, 133
    shades, *132*
Landscaping features,
    assessment of, 48
Lead paint, 141
Lead water supply lines, 128
Library, *104-105*
Light fixtures, *132*, 133
    and renovation, 150, *151*
    and restoration, *147*
Lintel, curved, *97*
Living/dining area in open
    plan, *78-79*
Living rooms
    adding on, *68-69*
    ceilings
        beamed, *66-67, 74*
        removal, *73, 99, 107,*
    doors, *111*
        French, *67*
        removed, *102*
    finishing/furnishing
        remodeled house,
            152-153
        renovated house, *151*
        restored house, *144*
    informal, library as, *104-105*
    row house, *74*
    stairways, new, *73, 108*
    two-family into one-family
        house, *76-77*
    wall removal, *98-101*
    windows, *110-111*
        wood trim, *117*
Loans, 45
Locks, replacing, 131
Loft in converted warehouse,
    14-15

M-P

Mantels
    marble, *113, 135*
    wood, *135*
Materials
    for renovation, 59, 80-81
    for restoration, 58-59
Mechanical systems, 41,
        118-129
    cooling, *119,* 121
    heating
        ducted, 41, *118-119,* 120
        piped, *49,* 120-121

Mechanical systems *(contd.)*
    plumbing, 41, *126-127,*
        128-129
    wiring, 41, *122-123,*
        124-125
Metal, pressed, *106,* 106-107,
    135
Millwork, 115
    contemporary, *116-117*
Moldings
    plaster, duplicating, 135
    pressed metal, *135*
    wood, re-creating, 136
Mold, rubber, for casting
    plaster, 135
Morris, William, wallpaper
    pattern inspired by, *140*
Mothballing of old house, 81
Moving of house, 72
Multipane versus single-pane
    windows, 137
Neighborhood
    checklist for, 36-37
    renewing, *82-83*
Neon test light, use of, 125
Oil and kerosene lamps, 133
Paint, 141
    for exteriors, *92-95*
        removing, 136
        restorations, 87
    lead, 141
Paneling, wood, *140,* 141
Passive cooling, 121
Piped heating systems, *49,*
    120-121
Pipe, plumbing, kinds of
    drain-waste-vent lines, 129
    supply lines, 128
Planes, molding, 136
Planning process, 46-65
    assessment of house, *48-49*
    costs, determining, 62-63
    design choices, final, *58-61*
    design process, *54-57*
    drawings of house
        professional, 54-55
        rough, preparing, *50-51*
    professionals, use of,
        54-55, 64-65
    renewal options, defined, 46
    wants, listing, *52-53*
    work, arranging for, 64-65
Plants, skylight-hung, *116*
Plaster detailing, *49*
    duplicating, 135

Plastic pipe for plumbing
    systems, 128, 129
Plastic-sheathed cable, 124
Plinth blocks, *114-115*
Plumbing hardware, 130-131,
    131
Plumbing systems, 41,
    126-127, 128-129
Porches
    gazebos, attached, *9, 87*
    restored, *84-85*
Preservation, defined, 46
Pressed metal, *106,* 106-107,
    135
Professionals, use of, 64-65
    drawings, kinds of, 54-55
Property taxes, 37

Q-R

Queen Anne gingerbread, *97*
Queen Anne style, *8-9, 24, 26*
Quick valve on radiator, 120
Radiators, *49*
    hot water, 120-121
    steam, 120
Rehabilitation. *See* Renovation
Remodeling
    case study, *66-67*
    furnishing, *152-154*
    row house, *74-75*
    wall and ceiling removal, *73,*
        98-101, 107
Renewal projects
    case studies, 66-83
        adding on, *68-69,* 80, *81*
        beautification, *72-73*
        converted shop, *78-79*
        farm, *80-81*
        neighborhood, *82-83*
        one-family from two-family
            house, *76-77*
        opening up, *66-67*
        past, re-creation of, *70-71*
        row house, *74-75*
    conversion of commercial
        buildings, *14-15,* 24,
        78-79
    details, 12, 130-141
        architectural, exterior,
            12-13, 96-97, 136-137
        architectural, interior,
            114-115, 134-135
        floors, wood, 138, *139*
        hardware, *130-131*

Renewal projects *(contd.)*
    details *(contd.)*
        lighting, *132,* 133
        wall treatments, *71, 140,*
            141
    disruption during, *17*
    financial considerations, 19,
        45
        costs, 62-63
        tax incentives, 75
    finishing and furnishing,
        142-154
        plans, 142, *143*
        remodeled house,
            152-154
        renovated house,
            148-151
        restored house, *144-147*
    house types
        farmhouses, *7,* 32, *34-35,*
            84-85, 92
        row houses, *18-19,* 22,
            23, 74-75
        small-town, *32-33*
        suburban, newer, *30-31,*
            152-154
        suburban, older, *28-29*
        See also Victorian homes
    interiors, 98-117
        ceiling treatments, *99,*
            106-107, 135
        details, *114-115, 134-135*
        old-new balance, *102-103*
        stairways, *73, 108-109*
        traffic plans, improving,
            105
        wall removal, *98-101*
        windows/doors, *110-111*
        woodwork, contemporary,
            116-117
        woodwork, old, *114-115*
        See also Fireplaces
    large-scale urban recycling,
        24-25
    location for, 20, 34
        neighborhood checklist,
            36-37
    materials for, 58-59, 80-81
    potential, identifying, 8
    research, 43
    restoration versus
        renovation, *10-11*
    search for house, 6
    visual inspection of home
        exterior, 38
        interior, 41

INDEX
(continued)

See also Exteriors,
    renewing; Mechanical
    systems; Planning
    process

Renovation, *11*
    costs, estimating, 63
    definiton, 46
    exterior
        ranch house, *90-91*
        with roof extension, *88-89*
    final design, example of, *61*
    furnishing, *148-151*
    materials for, 59, 80-81
    original house design,
        selective use of, 53
    planning. *See* Planning
        process
Rental properties, tax
    incentives for, 75
Reproduction furnishings, 146
Restoration
    case study, *70-71*
    costs, estimating, 62
    definition, 46
    exterior, *8-9, 21, 70, 84-87,*
        145
    final design, example of, *60*
    furnishing *144-147*
    guidelines, 71
    interpretive, *10,* 11, 52, 87
    materials for, 58-59
    planning. *See* Planning
        process
Romex (plastic-sheathed
    cable), 124
Roof extension, *89*
Roof inspection, 38
Room air conditioners, 121
Row houses, *18-19,* 22, *23,*
    74-75

S-Y

Salvage materials, buying, 81
Sanding versus stripping of
    floors, 138
Sawn-wood trim, 136
Schools, evaluating, 37
Services, community, 36-37
Shelves, wall-hung, *154*
Shingles for siding, *75, 88-89*
Shutoff valves for water
    supply lines, 128

Siding
    color, appropriate, *86, 95*
    plywood with battens, *90-91*
    shingles, *75, 88-89*
    shiplapped, restored, *84-85*
Sitting room, fireplace in, *113*
Skylights, *116*
Small-town cottages, *32-33*
Solarium, *148-149*
Stairways
    new, *73, 108*
    restoration, *109*
Steam heating systems, 120
Stenciling, 141
Stripping versus sanding of
    floors, 138
Suburban homes, types of
    newer, *30-31, 152-154*
    older, *28-29*
Supply lines, water, *126-127,*
    128-129
Taxes, property, 37
Tax incentives for rental
    properties, 75
Tile floor, *152,* 154
Town houses
    Georgian, *25*
    interior, *104-105*
    Victorian, *95*
Traffic plans, improving, *105*
Trim
    exterior
        accentuating, 92
        ornamental, *12-13, 96-97,*
        136
    interior, *114-115, 134-135*
Urethane moldings/trim, 135
U.S. Department of Interior
    standards, 48
Venting of plumbing, 129
Victorian homes, 27, *71,*
    144-147
    colors, 92
    entrance halls, *10, 147*
    exteriors, *22, 70, 75, 86, 93,*
        145
        Carpenter Gothic cottage,
        32-33
        farmhouse, *34-35*
        Italianate, *21, 27, 95*
        Queen Anne, *8-9, 24, 26*
    lighting styles, *132,* 133
    row house, *74-75*
    windows and doors, *111*
Wallpaper, *71, 140,* 141
Wall removal, *98-101*
Walls, exterior, inspecting, 38

Wall treatments, *140,* 141
    for Victorian homes, *71*
Warehouse, converted, *14-15*
Water supply lines, *126-127,*
    128-129
Water trapped in radiator, 120
Windows, *110-111*
    blinds, vertical, *152-153*
    exterior, 136-137, *137*
        bay, detailing around, *95*
    increased efficiency, need
        for, *49*
    leaded glass, *147*
    mullioned, *148*
    trim
        curvilinear, *97*
        wood, 116, *117*
Wiring, 41, *122-123,* 124-125
Wood exterior trim, renewing,
    136
Wood floors, 138, *139*
Wood mantel, *135*
Wood moldings, re-creating,
    136
Wood wireways, 124
Woodwork, *134*
    contemporary millwork,
        116-117
    old
        matching, 80-81
        paneling, *140,* 141
        restoring, *114-115*
Wrought-iron fence, *86*
Yards, assessment of, 48